Over My Dead Body!

A Workbook for Community Involvement

Lance Decker
Lindworth Press

Over My Dead Body!
A Workbook for Community Involvement

Cover Illustration: ATG Productions
Cover and Interior Design: The Printed Page

Second Edition
ISBN: 0-9710881-1-X

Published by
Lindworth Press
5135 North 41st Place
Phoenix, AZ 85018-1664
www.lldecker.com
www.communityinvolvement.org

Acknowledgments

This book is dedicated to all the hard working, over-taxed and under appreciated public employees who find the patience to put these concepts into day-to-day practice. These are optimistic people of good will, who, over the past 20 years, provided a learning laboratory for LL Decker & Associates. Without our sponsors and clients we never would have had the opportunity to apply our craft.

I want to acknowledge several of my colleagues and associates:

- Theresa Gunn, in 1996, helped write the original training manual on this subject documenting community involvement techniques.

- Ruth Yabes, PhD and faculty member at Arizona State University provided invaluable critique in preparing this second edition.

- Lou Weschler, PhD, now a retired professor from Arizona State University and my beloved mentor, introduced me to the power of qualitative research.

- Teresa Makinen, a good friend and great business manager supplied continuous logistical support.

- Jeanine Decker, my wife, gave me the extra time and encouragement I needed during some very trying times. Because of her I finally finished this second edition.

Contents

Chapter 6: Meetings and Their Role in Community Involvement

Chapter 7: Managing Conflict and Mediating Community Disputes

Foreword

A friend of mine once said, "It's really simple. When it comes to public policy, two factors determine how people feel...personal power and money. And if you believe that money is just a way of keeping score, then it's all about power." I pondered those words for a long time. That's a pretty strong indictment of democracy and the shallow, self-serving attitudes of our constituencies, public managers, elected officials and policy makers. We've all seen situations where it appeared an individual or group rejected the common good for personal gain. Is it that we can't put personal profit aside long enough to consider the collective benefit, or is it the fear of losing that little bit of control and power we believe we have that drives the conflict?

Helping people make good public decisions and then helping them make those decisions work is the subject of this book. The title came from a public hearing involving a wastewater treatment and recycling plant proposed in the center of a suburban community. As the city staff member finished his presentation requesting council approval, a woman in the back of the room shouted, "Over my dead body!" In those few words she established the tone of a debate that was to last eighteen months.

It isn't easy being a public official. Policy makers are responsible for decisions that, by their very nature, are controversial. They address critical public needs and wants. They use democratic principals as the litmus test. They must take the broadest, most inclusive perspective possible. This process takes time and doesn't come without

> *"Man's mind once stretched by a new idea, never regains its original dimensions."*
>
> —Oliver Wendell Holmes

"I once thought that our work enhanced the power of the public... but, in fact, the bureaucrat is the one that benefits most from community involvement. The bureaucrat benefits from the depth and breadth of intellectual capital that citizens represent. He benefits from the clarity of organization and direction that the agency must provide before it can effectively engage stakeholders. The bureaucrat benefits from the eventual quality of the decision and the wealth of support that community-based planning generates. The authority citizens accrue by being involved in public decisions pales when compared to the power generated by public agencies willing to invest in the human capital of its citizens."

—Lance Decker

criticism. When the decision is finally made, the official has had to balance not only the public good, but also the ephemeral concepts of fairness and justice.

This book was written to give public managers responsible for community involvement the tools to successfully do their jobs. The techniques outlined assume that decisions made in a democratic society are subject to disclosure, discussion and debate in a public forum, through a public process. Let all people hear, know and judge. It addresses the typical situations we find ourselves facing as we work through public issues. There will be instances where special communities and unique cultures require adaptation of the tools and techniques highlighted here, but, for the most part, these techniques have been effective in redirecting anger and encouraging issue resolution.

Throughout this book I've included stories, vignettes, checklists and pithy quotes to help the reader put into context the conceptual text. Because much of this material comes from 20 years of personal experience, I took the liberty of writing in the first person. Likewise, you occasionally will read a section that sounds like an instruction manual. That's because *it is* an instruction manual. Feel free to apply these techniques liberally, but with caution.

If you don't have time to read the rest of this book, remember the following seven items:

- Give **accurate, timely and appropriate information**; don't hide things pertinent to a public decision.

- Give people the **opportunity to do the right thing** without being forced to do so.

- Give everyone **a voice in the decisions** that affect them, and listen to what they say.

- Give everyone **respect**.

- Provide **choices**.

- **Don't manipulate** people or the community involvement process.

- No matter how heated the discussion gets...**preserve self-esteem**.

"All government—indeed, every human benefit and enjoyment, every virtue and every prudent act—is founded on compromise and barter."

—Edmund Burke

A conversation heard during a heated public meeting:

Agency representative: "How many times do we have to say 'no' before you understand that we mean 'no'?"

Community leader: "As many times as it takes to get you to say 'yes' and make it mean 'yes'!"

Introduction

Civic collaboration is a process of shared decision making in which all the parties with a stake in a problem constructively explore their differences and develop a joint strategy for action. The ethic of collaboration is premised on the belief that politics does not have to be a zero-sum game where one party wins and one party loses, or where both sides settle for a compromise. If the right people are brought together in constructive ways and with the appropriate information they can not only create authentic visions and strategies for addressing their joint problems but also, in many cases, overcome their limited perspectives of what is possible.

—Scott London, "Collaboration and Community", November, 1995,
   Pew Partnership for Civic Change

Orientation to Public Involvement

Shared responsibility and civic collaboration are the foundation of community-directed planning and involvement. Public officials and managers cannot provide all the services that a community might want, need or expect, and it is a disservice to that community for those persons to think they can. This book highlights the errors that occur when public officials and managers try to do everything for everyone, and illustrates the benefits of involving communities in the planning, research, decision making, and implementing process.

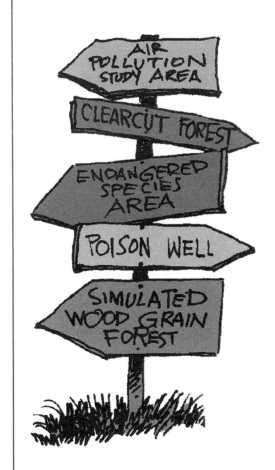

What's driving this movement toward community-based, collaborative decision making? It appears that pressure is coming from at least two directions.

First, government is being asked to provide more services, reduce taxes, increase fee-based revenue and become more efficient. To meet such a challenge, government must gain the support and cooperation of citizens for finding service alternatives and establishing priorities for limited resources. In addition, many government leaders believe that community members can provide personal energy and intellectual capital to their organizations. These are bright, energetic people who are often willing to contribute their treasury of great ideas to the public service if they are given a meaningful role.

Second, community members are demanding a meaningful role in the process of governance. They want to take control of their communities, participate in democratic processes, and find resolution to their own unique problems. By giving them the power to discuss, plan and decide their own futures, citizens acquire ownership of the decision, are more likely to abide by that decision and will find ways to make the decision work smoothly.

In most communities citizen participation is no longer an option...it's the law! Involving citizens in decisions that affect them is also the right thing to do.

"Some people strengthen the society just by being the kind of people they are."

—John Gardner

What You Need to Know about this Book

Purpose and Objectives of the Book

This book shows public officials, administrators and citizens how community involvement processes can benefit their jurisdictions, and how community members and public leaders can work together as allies and not enemies. Above all else, the book is a practical aid to understanding how community-based planning works. It answers the questions, "What can we gain from engaging in structured civic dialogue?" and "How might we proceed with such discussions?" It provides useful tools and techniques to determine the appropriate levels of community involvement necessary for a project or controversy, and illustrates the step-by-step methods for implementing community involvement. In the end, this book should be a starting point for building community capacity, solving community problems, and creating community partnerships.

The processes described in this book are currently being used broadly in North America, and the public involvement techniques described and illustrated in this book can make a difference in any town, city, county or state willing to use them consistently over the long term.

Organization of the Book

There are eight chapters, an introduction and four appendices in this book. Each chapter addresses a basic concept of community-based planning and involvement. Each chapter begins with an episode of the story of Chicken Grove. The appendices contains snapshots of forms used within the chapters to illustrate and support key concepts. Full-sized, downloadable copies of these forms can be obtained from the Institute for Community Involvement website at www.communityinvolvement.org.

- Chapter 1 is a basic orientation to the history, philosophy, and theory of community involvement.

- Chapter 2 introduces a five-stage step-by-step model for community involvement.

- Chapter 3 focuses on community-directed planning and intervention research.

- Chapter 4 highlights community involvement strategy and program design.

- Chapter 5 examines the community involvement deployment process showing how community-directed planning and involvement is implemented.

- Chapter 6 discusses meetings and how they enter into the community involvement process, highlights methods for managing meetings and public events, and provides detailed tools and techniques for communicating with and engaging stakeholders.

- Chapter 7 develops a series of techniques for managing personal conflicts within institutional settings, outlines methods for identifying and dealing with "snipers," and poses fundamental methods for mediating disputes.

- Chapter 8 is a guide to local capacity-building and self sufficiency for community involvement.

The Story of Chicken Grove

Chicken Grove's tale focuses on a group of people involved in collective decision making for a public purpose. It's the story of a fire station, a neighborhood, and a city. The characters in the story are people just like you. They have hopes and dreams, unique perspectives on change, fears, angers, and strongly held beliefs. It's the story of community-based, collaborative planning. Chicken Grove is the story of every city, town, county and state that values the democratic process and wants to honor their citizens, but doesn't know exactly how to do it.

The story of Chicken Grove involves many communities...a variety of stakeholders...opposing interests...and the fundamental changes that intrude on our lives. It concerns you, the socio-political environment in which you live, and the people you engage.

A new segment of Chicken Grove's struggle to build a fire station introduces each chapter of this workbook. The substantive topic developed in each chapter is highlighted in the story, and "driving questions" are posed about the story to put the story in context.

Chapter 1:

Theory and Philosophy of Community Involvement

The Story of Chicken Grove

Chicken Grove was founded in the late 1800's as a civic center supporting surrounding agricultural activities. Over the next 75 years Chicken Grove successfully grew to almost 6,000 people. It was known for its quiet, rural lifestyle and family values where everyone knew everyone else, and where neighbors were genuinely committed to each other. It was a stable community and if you were born in Chicken Grove, it was a good bet that you would remain there most of your life.

At the same time and about sixty miles away, the neighboring city of Turkey Crossing was founded. Turkey Crossing chose a different direction and became the trading and financial center for the region. It grew rapidly after World War II, and by 1970 it had a population in excess of 750,000. Its influence on the surrounding area became overwhelming and Turkey Crossing became the central city of the region, with Chicken Groove one of its bedroom communities.

Chicken Grove began to feel the power of suburban growth when its farmlands started to become new, large-scale residential developments. A freeway cut across its northern border making access easier and quicker, so by 1980

Chicken Grove's population had doubled. The congestion, crime, housing deterioration and industrial pollution of the central city sent waves of families looking for a better place to live. By 1990 Chicken Grove had over 50,000 people, and that kind of rapid growth created both opportunities and difficulties for the town, its residents, its schools and its businesses. Chicken Grove wasn't like it used to be...and that concerned a whole lot of folks.

Questions to Frame Discussion

Public managers and community leaders need to ask several critical questions about the history and context of their communities and how public involvement might support governance.

- How does Chicken Grove define itself as a community?

- What complaints might "old-timers" have about the changes anticipated in Chicken Grove?

- What distinct and unique communities might you find in Chicken Grove?

- In what ways does Chicken Grove's past have an impact on its future?

What is Community Involvement?

Community involvement is a collaborative effort between governments and the communities they serve to identify and resolve problems, or to capitalize on opportunities. The objective is to engage all people who might want a voice in a decision or problem in the search for and implementation of solutions. By devising mutually beneficial ties between policy makers, public managers and staff, and community members, this process has become an accepted technique for addressing the changes facing our society.

Progressive communities all around the world are initiating community involvement to bring citizens, leaders, and public officials into structured, win-win discussions to resolve issues and manage problems. Community involvement seeks to develop consensus on the actions that citizens and local governments must take to survive and prosper. Community involvement drives planning toward action with the dual partnership of public citizenry and government officials. This association precipitates a smoother assembly of community resources and develops community partnerships that give most, if not all, participants a fulfilling role in resulting efforts. Having said all that, we need to be clear. The public participation and community involvement discussed in this workbook is not public relations. There is no attempt to "sell" or "market" public policies to an unsuspecting community.

What *does* Pareto Optimality mean to a public official?

Named after **Vilfredo Pareto**, *Pareto optimality* is a measure of **efficiency**. An outcome of a decision that meets the standard of being "Pareto optimal" is when there is no other outcome that makes every stakeholder at least as well off and at least one player strictly better off. That is, a Pareto Optimal outcome cannot be improved upon without hurting at least one stakeholder.

Public officials are responsible for making decisions that address critical public issues. In doing so, they try to help as many people as possible while minimizing the number of people who will lose by their decision.

Community Involvement Theory

Three concepts are critical to understanding why public involvement works so well. These concepts show why community planning is such a natural extension of these techniques.

> *First, people affected by public decisions need accurate information regarding those decisions, need a voice in those decisions, and need the opportunity to help determine how those decisions will be implemented.*

Most public managers and policy leaders would subscribe to this concept without thinking about the consequences. Few people in authority in the United States or Canada would publicly say the government needs to censor the truth, overtly lie about a problem or project, keep people from knowing about pending actions, limit conversations, and not allow citizens the opportunity to comment on or criticize a government action. Our Constitution protects those freedoms...our laws enforce compliance.

The depth and breadth of information a citizen obtains on a subject can vary widely from jurisdiction to jurisdiction. Being truthful doesn't necessarily mean being forthright and candid. In some situations citizens must go to court to obtain the full measure of information about a project or problem, resulting in a breach of trust with their government. High quality community-based involvement means that timely and accurate information is provided to any stakeholder (whether requested or not) in a form that aids understanding of the issues at hand.

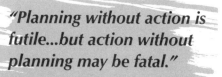

"Planning without action is futile...but action without planning may be fatal."

—Anonymous

Second, if people who are affected by a decision are involved in the process of policymaking, they will find ways to improve the quality of the decisions, will actively support the final policies, and will suggest methods to improve implementation of those policies.

The concept of decision "ownership" is common to both business and government. It is fair to say that people have an emotional commitment to things they own. As a tangible illustration, cars purchased by teenagers with their own hard-earned money are probably given better care than the ones loaned to them by their parents.

An example is a new 20-acre park to be located in a developing part of town. If the decisions to build it and the details of design have had broad, substantive involvement from the surrounding community, the park will more likely gain strong support. Conversely, if the community is left out of the decision, the simple act of exclusion will generate resentment from those affected by it.

Third, people adversely affected by a decision will be less likely to oppose the policy if they are given full information and their voices are heard and recognized.

Continuing with the example of a new 20-acre park, those people who directly border on the park may feel adversely affected. Bright lights will burn late into the evening, strangers will park in front of their homes, children will cut through their yards, dogs will...well, you get the picture. If the jurisdiction gives the area residents who are against the park an opportunity to voice their concerns, these discussions might generate remedies for some of the difficulties created. In this way, their time was well spent in raising the issues. Even if nothing can be done to ease the effects of the park, those against the park will have had their "day in court" and will feel that due process was given. They may still resent the decision to build the park, but they will be less likely to actively resist its development if they believe that a democratic process was followed.

Definition of Terms

Here are some definitions that may prove helpful when reading this workbook:

People

Agency, jurisdiction, organization, policy body all refer to the public sector institution formally responsible for initiating and organizing a public involvement process. A village, town, city, county, state, Native American community, taxing district, province, or borough could all be charged with conducting community involvement.

Community means any group of people who share a common interest, a common belief or a common investment in the future.

Community leaders are stakeholders who command the respect, loyalty and admiration of the individuals and groups with which they hold affiliation.

Participant, stakeholder, and resident all refer to the people to whom a public involvement process is directed. They are individuals, organizations, agencies, or political entities having an interest in the outcome of a project, problem or issue.

> *"Friends may come and friends may go, but a good enemy can last you a lifetime."*
>
> —Hagar the Horrible

Project manager is the person responsible for conducting an actual public involvement process or project.

Staff refers to people inside the organization who act in support of public involvement and who are responsible for deploying the process.

Sniper refers to a potential participant in a community involvement process who is an active adversary of the process.

Sponsor is the term used for people or organizations that formally convene a public involvement process. This could be a mayor, county supervisor, governor or other elected official. It could also mean an appointed official such as a city manager, department or division director, commissioner, or county administrator.

Focus of Activity

Problem, issue, project, decision, discussion, controversy, complaint, question, dilemma, difficulty, predicament and *opportunity* are all terms used to describe the reason for initiating a public involvement process.

Issue (question, controversy) is a point, matter or dispute of special or public importance; a trend or event, arising inside or outside an organization that can have an important influence on the organization's ability to reach its desired future. Issues arise when something or someone, either inside or outside the policy body, is proposing a change that the policy body may be responsible for deciding.

"At issue" is the crux of a dispute, which, if identified, can lead to discussion, option identification and issue resolution; in reference to the individual foundation elements comprising the overall issue, as in "what really is at issue is...".

(People in conflict or under stress may not take time to carefully analyze and articulate their fundamental concerns, or may couch those concerns in a politically correct or vague manner. For instance, a person may state that "the water treatment plant is noisy" even though the facility is well within noise limits. The real objection to the plant may be the color of the exterior walls, but wall color may not seem sufficient to lodge a complaint or give standing to an objection.)

Problems (controversy, question, dilemma, difficulty, predicament) occur where something has already happened that the policy body either caused, or the policy body has some regulatory or administrative authority to affect.

Project can mean either 1) a planned and coordinated community involvement process, 2) a physical structure or government program that will create (or has created) concern from potentially affected interests, citizens, residents or stakeholders, or 3) a planning process for land use, long-range services, and regional activities.

Opportunity is a proactive approach to planning for the future.

Processes and Process Components

Collaboration — Seeking partnership with others; cooperative, collective agreements that create benefit for all parties involved.

Community-based or community-directed planning is carefully searching for and involving stakeholders and potentially affected interests in the process of planning for their future. By adding the term "planning" to the word "community" we assume that the subject in question isn't a crisis, that there is time to methodically conduct a community involvement process.

Community involvement is the generic term used to describe the process public agencies use to engage people in civic dialogue. For purposes of this text, the terms citizen participation, public involvement, and public participation all mean the same thing: actively soliciting a broad and diverse mix of potential stakeholders in the process of discussing and deciding public issues.

Consensus describes a conditional decision made in a group setting, or a group process used to find agreement. Consensus may include:

● Mutual agreement that addresses the central issues but may not address every concern or be perfect from every possible perspective. In a consensus, the level of agreement is not usually perfect but is acceptable enough to the consenting parties to allow the process to proceed.

● A process that generates a decision which some members may not feel is the best one, but after discussion, one they can all agree is the best current direction, and they can live with, support, and commit to, without undermining.

Public involvement consultants initially work with clients in response to a need for intervention. If things work well, a subsequent program of community involvement and capacity building is the result.

● A process where decisions are arrived at without voting.

(Occasionally when the level of consensus is thin, people will refer to the decision as having "informed" or "grudging" consent.)

Development — An action or event that signals the organization that an issue is forthcoming. Also referred to as a "trigger."

Hyper vigilant refers to superficial scanning for the most obvious response to escape an immediate danger, at the expense of a more fundamental issue.

Intervention is the act of redirecting unproductive discussions that occur between two or more stakeholders, or between stakeholders and public authorities, toward responsible issue resolution; an act or activity designed to influence attitudes and align people's direction in terms of developing consensus or fundamental agreement on a course of action.

Organizational ideals are the fundamental beliefs and values held by an organization that gives it strategic direction and drives issue identification, analysis and resolution.

Public involvement means actively soliciting a broad and diverse mix of people in the process of discussing and deciding about public issues; a process or strategy for integrating the views of different publics into the decision-making process. (See *community involvement.*)

Paradox is the contradiction between two defensible interpretations of a position or idea. The arguments posed for each interpretation are cogent, but when put together they become contradictory.

Salience is the degree to which an issue is relevant, important and popular in the perception of stakeholders and the public.

Tractability is the prospect that an issue can be successfully addressed.

Linking Community-Based Planning, Community Involvement and Crisis Intervention

Unfortunately, public agencies constantly find themselves reacting to (intervening in) a community's cry for access to the decision during the process or after a decision has been made. Once a community feels a need to demand access, the term "crisis intervention" might be more accurate in describing activities. The process for undertaking community-based planning and involvement falls into five distinct stages.

The first stage is pre-planning. Pre-planning brings agency leaders together to:

1) Agree that public involvement is needed.
2) Outline the objectives of the public involvement process.
3) Develop timetables.
4) Create protocols and procedures to help all those involved understand their roles.
5) Identify the chain of command.
6) Establish project boundaries.

"The Plan was nothing, but the act of planning was everything."

General Dwight D, Eisenhower commenting on the invasion of Normandy

The second stage is research. Research identifies:

1) Critical stakeholders.
2) Specific issues that might be raised.
3) Specific stakeholders' perceptions of the issues.
4) Polarities and gaps that exist between the various stakeholder communities.
5) Possible methods to de-polarize contentious issues.

The third stage is strategy development and process design. During this stage the research findings are analyzed, and procedures are developed to address concerns. Process design matches communities and critical stakeholders to the tools and techniques that can best help them discuss and decide those issues. Potential design factors that might be considered could include the availability of human resources, the project's budget, gaps in public understanding, alternative communications methods, and the intensity of conflicts between opposing communities.

The fourth stage is systems implementation and process deployment. As the name implies, the agency applies their resources to help communities understand what is "at issue" and aid stakeholders in achieving the project goals. During the deployment stage agency staff are encouraged to assess progress and adapt/modify the basic approach to better serve all stakeholder interests.

The fifth stage is process review, ongoing planning and capacity building. During the community-based planning and involvement process the agency has learned much about the communities and key stakeholders. It would be unfortunate to lose this understanding, so this stage institutionalizes final data analysis. Staff reviews the process from start to finish and analyzes what strategies, techniques, and process steps helped the group achieve its desired outcomes. Likewise, if there were difficulties or "pot holes" in the process, they are identified and recorded. Based on this information, the agency can create an ongoing public involvement strategy. Each assessment adds information and capacity to the organization's ability to continuously, successfully engage and involve community interests.

When to Use Community Involvement Processes, Tools and Techniques

There are times when it is clearly in the jurisdiction's interest to use a full-blown community-based planning and involvement process. At other times, only some of the tools and techniques described in this book will be needed. Since these techniques are not without cost, it is important to know when to use a full set of involvement methods and when limited involvement is sufficient.

As a rule, the five-stage community involvement method is initiated when:

1) Clear direction on a significant public issue or community problem is not evident,

2) A project or policy will be perceived to negatively affect one or more community interests,

3) The costs and benefits of either success or failure are high,

4) Significant community capacity can be developed through the community involvement process, and/or

"Leadership is the willingness to expend political capital to meet a challenge."

—Anonymous

Benefits

- More effective end results
- Greater success in completing projects
- Less criticism from policy makers in the long run
- Responsibility shared with the community
- Increased trust and credibility in the organization
- Personal support from individuals
- Overall support for institutional goals
- Community skill building, leadership and capacity building
- Increased communication and respect between the organizations and stakeholder communities

5) There is enough interest to generate significant participation.

If, after completing the research stage of the initial process, information indicates a more limited community involvement approach is sufficient, then use only those community involvement tools necessary and sufficient to achieve the project or decision objectives.

Costs and Benefits of Community Involvement

Community involvement generates many positive outcomes for both the agency and the community, but those benefits do not come without a cost. The expenditure of staff resources and lots of hard work should be expected. There are also some serious downsides and limitations to the techniques highlighted in this book.

Benefits

When used properly, a well designed community involvement process will generate more effective results. Projects will look better, operate better and have higher levels of acceptance. Projects that could have been overwhelmed with public resistance will see more approval. In the long run, policy makers will see the wisdom of working within a community-based planning framework and use the techniques as part of standard procedures.

Responsibility for project development and performance will be shared with the communities engaged in decision making. Even projects and decisions that generate only modest controversy will benefit from a sense of shared community ownership.

There will be increased trust and credibility in the agency, in the organization, and in the individuals using these techniques. As a result and over the long run, support for institutional goals will be improved. Capacity within the community for civil discourse, leadership and governance is expanded, and a deeper, more meaningful communications network within and between stakeholder communities develops.

Costs

Where there are benefits, there are usually costs. Most projects and decisions will take longer to complete. Where once a jurisdiction would simply make the decision to locate a wastewater treatment plant based on geology and hydrology, now a complicated mix of socio-political and demographic factors come into play. Add to that already complicated process time for a meaningful discussion with the surrounding neighbors, and the project may go on for years.

As project critics and staff find ways to mitigate problems, they increase the initial capital costs and ongoing maintenance costs. The time extensions and delays that go with public involvement discussions add to project inflation.

Managers who use community involvement techniques may receive criticism from elected officials and policy makers early in the process. "Hey, we hired you to make decisions...not ask the town troublemakers for their opinions!" Often mayors and council members feel they were elected to make decisions, and that's what they're going to do. "If citizens want to make decisions, let them run for office next time!"

Costs

- Extended decision time
- Higher capital and maintenance costs
- Potential for criticism from elected officials and interest groups
- Challenge to professional standards
- Change in agency role
- View that community comment is interference
- Increased staff resources and costs
- Involvement used as delay tactic

Professional managers may be challenged by the community to rethink standard operating procedures. "Don't tell me why you can't do anything about that ugly water tank. Make it compatible with my neighborhood. Think of ways to make it unobtrusive." Professional standards and opinions mean almost nothing to a community leader who doesn't understand the profession.

Making projects more compatible with community needs may require higher capital and operating costs. For example, busses that create less pollution require special engines and fuel. In the long run benefits accrue by using more environmentally sensitive equipment, but the additional up-front costs may be significant. Likewise, intersections with left-turn arrows are popular with neighborhoods, but costly to city street departments.

There will be significant changes in the way agency staff perceives citizens. The "public servant, public citizen" relationship has changed over the past 20 years. Now, most jurisdictions look at residents as "customers" and public employees as "service providers." In the future, public agencies and stakeholders may become "partners." This willingness by public managers to allow citizens to view and comment on a wide range of public management systems will take time and will not be without serious discussions. Change does not come easily.

Public officials, both elected and appointed, may use a public involvement process as a delay tactic to slow, defer or even avoid a decision or project.

If you are planning for one year, grow rice. If you are planning for 20 years, grow trees. If you are planning for centuries, grow people.

—Chinese Proverb

The Dark Side of Public Involvement

Limitations to public involvement need to be acknowledged. Public involvement gives all people desiring access to a decision a voice in the discussion, whether they have legitimate standing as a stakeholder or not. A person or organization ("sniper") having no interest in resolving a particular local issue may use a public involvement opportunity to gain media attention for broader issues. A candidate for public office could use the community involvement process as a springboard to develop supporters. Don't be surprised when individuals use public events for personal and professional gain rather than problem solving.

Truly visionary projects may not make it through a comprehensive public involvement process. Hoover Dam was an inspiring project during the depression days of the 1930's, but would find it rough going in today's environmentally sensitive climate. New, untested technologies may be too risky and subject to significant public scrutiny. Anything that increases taxes is suspect and open to criticism.

A Costly but Effective Compromise

Desert communities work hard to manage their water. Building storage reservoirs on elevated sites means adequate water pressure at the kitchen sink. The bad news is the Brown Mesa subdivision is at the end of the current main. The good news is the town's water department had acquired a small mountain site just west of Brown Mesa on which to place a new two million gallon water tank.

As the bulldozer approached the mountain to start construction, workers found residents chained across the road. TV cameras were rolling, media reporters were on the scene. Their attorney had an injunction. All work came to a halt. "Wow," the project manager exclaimed, "these protestors are really organized!"

The engineering firm realized that delays like this hurt everyone. A meeting would have to be organized quickly to try to resolve the issues. The newspapers indicated that the protestors were upset about environmental damage to the mountain, plants and wildlife, fearful of the tank rupturing and destroying their homes, and worried about possible reduction in property values. "We just thought they wanted higher water pressure," said the water department director to the TV cameras.

At the meeting the contractor asked community leaders, "What's really wrong? We don't understand. We can move the trees and plants, give the squirrels new nests and make sure the birds aren't bothered. There is no reason to fear catastrophic tank failure… can't happen. If you'd like we can even bury half of the tank in the mountain to keep the profile in line with the geology of the area."

A buzz came from the protestors; that last statement got a reaction. "In fact," one of the protestors quietly admitted, "if the tank was partially buried, it might help matters." The group's unstated issue was the reservoir's horrible appearance.

Sensing a break through, the contractor continued. "What if we were to paint the concrete to match the mountain and throw some landscaping in to hide it? Will that do it?" Smiles came to the faces of many group members, but a few were not willing to let go that easy. "What else can you do?"

The engineers, contractor and water department rep huddled for awhile. Then came the reply, "What if we constructed a hard top on the tank and put a tennis court up there for the neighborhood?" Well, that did it.

Unfortunately, the cost of the project rose by 40% and the ongoing maintenance keeps staff hopping, but the water pressure problem was solved and the community was happy with their new facility.

Manipulation of the process by all sides in a dispute is possible. Agency staff, political and elected officials can create an unbalanced playing field. Community interests, using guerrilla tactics, can ambush and seize control of the meetings. Special interests working behind the scenes can disrupt and discredit the hard work of many honorable participants. Snipers, working outside the rules binding the formal group, can perform end runs to political interests, submit misleading and erroneous stories to the local media, and distribute materials containing outright falsehoods.

During the 1995 conference of the International Association for Public Participation (IAP2), practitioners were polled as to how frequently they were asked to manipulate a public involvement process or do something they thought was unethical. The results were surprising. Most respondents said they had, at one time or another, been asked to:

1) Tone down or omit controversial subjects in a fact sheet,

2) Ignore certain issues or concerns because the stakeholders were "irrational" or uninformed,

3) Encourage participation by stakeholders who were sympathetic to a project,

4) Withhold information that would reflect badly on a project, and/or

5) Exclude certain stakeholders from a public forum because their views did not support a project.

Words have Power

Make people accountable for their words. When a participant violates an element of the code of conduct involving inappropriate comments, don't let it pass unchallenged. Ask the violator, "What's going on? What's that about?" Once the group knows they will be accountable for their words, they will be less likely to violate the contract.

Because public involvement is a powerful tool and can be easily misused by both public agencies and by special interest groups, the IAP2, after two years of consultation with public participation practitioners, developed core values to guide community involvement program design and implementation. Due to copyright protections imposed by IAP2 on their materials, we will not reproduce them in this workbook, but you may view a number of excellent examples of public involvement tools and materials at the IAP2 website: www.iap2.org.

Things to Remember

- Community involvement is not difficult. The concepts are simple, easy to follow and relatively linear.

- Not all projects require or benefit from community involvement.

- Involve anyone who has a stake in the discussion.

- Community involvement will help expand valuable community resources.

- There is a cost to using community involvement processes.

Chapter 2:

Planning the Process

The Story of Chicken Grove

Chicken Grove needed a new fire station. The process for siting new public facilities was outlined in the town's standard operating procedures (SOP). The SOP's included the state's requirement for public notice and hearings. Chicken Grove always included citizens in decision making, and this time was no different. Fire Chief Harry Brown compiled a list of people who would make good representatives for a new ad hoc fire station site location committee. His selection strategy was to try to get someone from each of the five council districts and a handful of other folks who would support his recommendations. Harry really wanted to get the most qualified people he could, but it was important that they attend meetings during the day so the Fire Department wouldn't have to pay staff overtime for evening work. He knew the drill and believed if he selected the right people he could get through this process quickly.

Since it was a fire station he wanted to build, Harry found a retired fire fighter that lived in Chicken Grove to serve as a technical expert. The business community needed to be involved since nothing happens in Chicken Grove without the Chamber of Commerce support. The old time farm interests were still a powerful force. If a venerable former state senator and the wife of the

pastor of the largest church in town were involved it would give the group undisputed credibility. So after many phone calls, Harry had his ten-member committee. Harry submitted his list for the ad hoc committee to the Mayor and Council for their approval and adoption which he received without comment.

Harry's public involvement strategy was simple. He would assemble the committee and give them their assignment. The group would elect a chair that would work with Harry and the staff. Staff would review the data gener- ated by the computer model, conduct any additional research that seemed appropriate, do a preliminary evaluation of the fire station location, and submit the alternatives to the committee for their review and comments. Staff would gather more information about the final recommended sites. They would send that information back to the group so that the committee could make a final recommendation. The plan would then be sent to the Town Council for final adoption.

In fact, this is exactly how the process was conducted.

What's wrong?

What's wrong with Chief Harry's public involvement model? On the surface it seems rigorous enough since it includes lots of people, lots of meetings, and significant research. So then why will it all blow up in the Town Council Chambers?

Chief Harry had conducted these citizen participation processes many times before, and felt that nothing had changed. But, in fact, things in Chicken Grove are changing, and had Chief Harry conducted community-based research, he would have known that his process was flawed and inadequate.

Questions to Frame Discussion

The following questions should be reviewed prior to reading this next chapter. They raise some critical concerns that Harry and his staff should have considered before embarking on a community involvement process.

- What is the issue or challenge that the project needs to address? What is "at issue?"

- Does everyone agree that there's a problem? Do they see the problem the same way?

- Who are the people directly or indirectly affected by the project?

- What are the project's goals/objectives?

- What will happen if no action is taken?

- What are the anticipated project milestones?

- What is the current status of the issue, challenge or project?

- What is the purpose of involving the community in this project?

- Are there any community resources currently available for project implementation?

- What kinds of public involvement activities might be helpful?

The Community Involvement Process

The objectives of public participation are to give anyone seeing themselves as stakeholders:

- Timely, accurate and appropriate information about the issues, and
- A voice in the process.

By striving for these objectives, understanding and ownership of the decision will improve chances of finding a better resolution to problems and advance implementation of projects. A successful community involvement process design will support such objectives.

A basic process design can be successfully completed using a relatively simple linear process. It is not difficult, but a number of sequential steps must be followed.

Chapter One highlighted five stages of community involvement:

1. Pre-planning

2. Research

3. Strategic Development / Process Design

4. Systems Implementation / Process Deployment

5. Process Review and Ongoing Planning

The process starts with initial pre-process planning and research. After research is completed and analyzed, a decision is made to either proceed with a full-blown public involvement process, or scale back the effort using selected tools and techniques. Whether using a complete or limited approach, the process is implemented. Action planning starts the implementation stage and interim progress checks are completed as the process moves forward. Once all planned activities are completed, the entire community involvement process is reviewed, analyzed and documented. This "autopsy" (review, debriefing, etc.) sets the stage for future public involvement efforts, and builds capacity within the community for additional civil discourse.

The Five Stages of Community Involvement

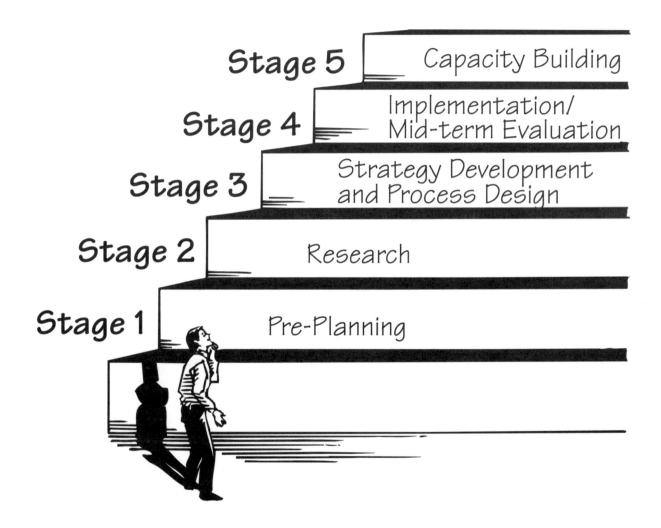

Stage 5 — Capacity Building

Stage 4 — Implementation/ Mid-term Evaluation

Stage 3 — Strategy Development and Process Design

Stage 2 — Research

Stage 1 — Pre-Planning

Stage 1: Pre-Planning

Before any design work can begin, the project team needs to determine if community involvement is really necessary by asking some critical questions. *Is there anything about this project or decision that is controversial? Are there potentially affected interests? Are there any unrecognized issues, collateral matters or ancillary activities that may make this project or decision vulnerable to criticism? Can the project or decision be significantly improved if citizens are tapped for their input?*

It is important to know when and when not to use community involvement. Sometimes issues and problems can be resolved simply by asking individuals to act independently. If public involvement is used unnecessarily, it loses impact, raises false expectations, creates undue controversy and wastes resources. So, if community involvement is not necessary, don't use it.

Likewise, don't ask the community to comment when a decision has already been discussed and made, is intuitively obvious to anyone, or when there are no reasonable alternatives. Example: If a waterline to the only elementary school in town breaks during the winter, is there really any alternative to making repairs? Probably not, and asking for public input would waste time and prompt criticism.

However, when an issue or problem cannot be resolved by unilateral action, then some level of community involvement may be

Stage 1: Pre-Planning

- Determine if public involvement is needed or desired

- Decide what level of involvement is appropriate

- Develop a draft "think piece" of what public involvement might look like

- Establish process objectives and boundaries

- Establish authority and responsibility for the process

- Establish discrete deliverables and expectations

- Address internal resistance to involvement

- Establish project reporting relationships

- Develop timetables

- Define the substantive issues

- Create an initial project team

"A carelessly planned project will take three times longer to complete than expected. A carefully planned project will only take twice as long."

—Golub's Law

helpful. Project sponsors, agency managers and the project staff all must be involved in this part of the process to determine if the issue, project, problem or decision will benefit from public involvement.

Level of Involvement

If it is decided that public involvement is important and should be undertaken, then the next decision is "what level of involvement is appropriate?" Is simple public notification and a few neighborhood meetings all that's needed, or is a city-wide process required to assure full stakeholder assessment and involvement? Each optional level should have a set of draft objectives developed. There are probably a limited number of active community partners for any particular issue, so use their time wisely.

Draft Community Involvement Plan

Once a need for and level of community involvement is determined, a draft plan to engage people becomes necessary. This "think piece" might include a list of internal agency actors who should be involved, a basic timetable for performance, possible involvement methods, how cooperation and collaboration between the project staff and the public might occur, and potential resources for implementing the plan.

Boundaries

Project boundaries simply tell everyone involved where they can and cannot go, and what they are open to discuss in conducting their work. For instance, if the decision to "direct the City Treasurer to invest excess, short-term tax monies in interest bearing accounts" has already been adopted, why would the Mayor ask a citizen committee to study whether the City Treasurer should do it? Rather, instruct the Committee to determine how such investments might best be made. Boundaries can apply to both process and substance.

Authority and Responsibility

All people serving in an advisory capacity want to know what topics are open for advice and what authority the participants have to act. Levels of authority and responsibility for both agency actors and citizens in the process must be determined as early as possible. Is the objective of the process to simply inform the public, or do citizens have a role in decision making?

Deliverables and Expectations

Successful citizen/community involvement efforts create clear, unambiguous process outcomes and reasonable expectations. This does not mean that the agency determines in advance of deploying the process what the substantive recommendations will be. Rather the group should establish the process outcomes they want to achieve. A statement such as, *At the conclusion of this process the Advisory Committee will make recommendations on ways the City Treasurer can increase the net income from investments and maintain a conservative investment portfolio,* establishes clear deliverables.

Overcoming Resistance to Involvement

Often public officials are skeptical of what residents and stakeholders might contribute to a project. They are cautious about letting outsiders look too closely into their internal affairs. Typically public managers feel the only time community

"To get maximum attention, it's hard to beat a great, big mistake."

—Anonymous

members are interested in what they do is when they want to find fault, look for corruption or criticize their operations. Unfortunately these past perceptions may have been true.

To overcome this resistance to community involvement, it helps to set clear boundaries. "The discussion of how the finance department invests taxes they receive until those taxes are needed will be limited to general property taxes...and does not include water revenues." This is a way to give focus to the inquiry while assuring the Treasurer that an overly-zealous community member won't use this as an excuse for a witch hunt.

Reporting Relationships

Who, from the sponsoring agency, calls the shots? Who decides when and where to hold a meeting, and specifically whom to invite? Identifying reporting relationships early in the community involvement process will ensure a smooth and seamless team effort. A list of communities and leaders is imperative for a successful outcome to the project. The people on this list should:

- Make good partners and be willing to work together.
- Represent a balanced group and a cross-section of interests.
- Muster community resources.
- Make decisions that will stick.
- Be "doers" as well as "thinkers."

Timetables

The first round of time estimates for any project will serve only as a starting point. When estimates are updated, new copies of the estimates need to be distributed to all members of the project to keep people in the loop and avoid surprises.

Issue Definition

The most important as well as the most difficult task of the design process is defining issues. Take time to carefully consider what the crux issue is. Determining what is "at issue" isn't always as easy as it first seems. Once the critical issues vital to the group's discussion are discovered, a statement must be crafted that accurately reflects the outcomes being sought.

As soon as possible after deciding to undertake a community-based involvement process, put the outcomes and objectives in writing. These outcomes and objectives should be shared with the other project partners so they can be modified, adjusted and clarified, as necessary. The objectives need to fit everyone's agenda. Objectives shared by all will become everyone's priority.

Create an Initial Project Team

The initial project team should include community leaders as well as internal staff from the sponsor agency. Select a relatively small group of people with a stake in conducting an honest, balanced and successful process. Avoid selecting people with parochial or self-serving interests if possible. This initial project team may not continue to be active in the public involvement implementation process, but will provide the input to build a firm process foundation.

Stage 2: Research

- Develop a research design
- Conduct research
- Analyze data

Stage 2: Research

Community research is necessary to determine what beliefs, perceptions, feelings and understandings the various stakeholder communities have about issues at hand. Such qualitative research can provide an early warning of possible difficulties and opportunities. Research can also be used to give participants information. By conducting community-based research the agency supports the philosophy of accurate, timely and appropriate levels of information for all stakeholders.

Questions to start the research process for stakeholders might include:

1. Is the problem, project, issue or decision salient? Do people recognize the importance of dealing with and discussing the topic?

2. Is the problem, project, issue or decision perceived to be tractable by stakeholders? Is there really anything to discuss? Is direction self-evident; are there really choices? Can anybody do anything about the issue?

3. Is the timing right? Are stakeholders ready to find a resolution or make a decision?

4. Which specific communities are ready to take action and where do they stand on issues?

5. What polarity exists and how might a public involvement process reduce this polarity?

6. What potential methods might a jurisdiction, agency or sponsor use to help these stakeholder groups resolve issues?

7. Who should be involved?

Things are always changing in Mount Adams. The town once had a prosperous gold mine, but when the price of minerals dropped and the quality of ore declined, people moved away. Fortunately for the town's residents, the beautiful mountains and fresh air attracted another type of prospector: Retirees. The homes that formerly belonged to the mine were acquired by new arrivals on fixed incomes who wanted to live far away from the cities. That was fifty years ago.

Now, with new technologies for processing ore and an increase in gold prices, mining in Mount Adams is being reconsidered. In fact, the New Venture Mining Company recently bought the land and mineral rights to reopen operations. Can you believe that there are people in town that aren't overwhelmingly pleased? In fact, there's a whole lot of talk about sabotaging the trucks and equipment if New Venture tries to open the mine again. It seems that the people who now live in Mount Adams don't want a gold mine in their back yard.

To find out how much trouble there might really be, the company hired a community involvement consulting firm to conduct research. The company needed to know how intense local residents are in their opposition to the mine, and what their concerns are. And, if they are against opening the mine, how hard will they fight to keep it from opening?

In a small community like Mount Adams, where would you start the research process?

The local tavern or restaurant is a good place to begin. More than likely, someone will start a conversation with "Where are you from?" or "What are you doing here?" An honest reply can be returned such as, "I'm interested in finding out how people feel about the proposed gold mine. Got any ideas?" The town barber is another resource for taking the pulse on the debate.

Lesson: It's surprising what folks will tell you if you just ask. Don't push… just ask.

Community research identifies the key stakeholder communities and the issues specific to the proposed project. Research also gauges stakeholders' perceptions of the issues and how intensely those perceptions are held. By asking critical players to reflect on their feelings, the sponsor starts the issue resolution process even in advance of the first formal meeting. The objective is to gain an understanding of what is on the stakeholders' minds and give the people managing the process information and a possible set of alternatives.

The direct benefit of this research is primarily to the project sponsor, but there are collateral benefits that accrue to everyone in the process. By determining the scope, depth and breadth of the discussions, meetings can be more timely and efficient. Defining issue polarity and information gaps means that the stakeholders can move quickly through issues that are of little substantive consequence. By one group simply acknowledging that another group has a legitimate concern gives everyone a place at the table and a voice in the discussion. After reviewing the research findings, most process participants will start de-polarizing marginal issues and start focusing on only those issues most relevant and contentious to the discussion. Research can also help keep the "temperature" of the debate under control.

Whether using full-blown public involvement or a scaled-back version, community research must be conducted prior to the start of the formal process. This is done to gather intelligence data from potentially affected interests and to give critical stakeholders accurate, timely and appropriate information.

Research should identify significantly affected communities, the overt and covert leadership within those communities, and the strategic issues that will affect the direction of the project. The results that come from community research help

> *What convinces is conviction. Believe in the argument you are advancing. If you don't, you're as good as dead. The other person will sense something isn't there and no chain of reasoning, no matter how logical or elegant or brilliant, will win your case for you.*
>
> —Lyndon B. Johnson

elected officials and policymakers clearly see the barriers they face before proceeding.

Typical Research Techniques

Three research techniques are typically used in community involvement. All three types focus on qualitative (feelings, beliefs, perceptions) research as opposed to quantitative (counting numbers, votes) research.

Issue mapping   Either formal or informal, issue mapping is used to systematically analyze communities and their leaders. It is a highly structured, three-tiered process that is relatively expensive in terms of staff time, but is thorough, reliable and generally inconspicuous. Issue mapping obtains the best, most usable information for public involvement purposes, and can be scaled to fit almost any circumstance. Informal issue mapping can also be used to gather information that may be difficult to obtain any other way.

Focus groups   Often helpful in starting the issue resolution process, focus groups create a much higher profile because they involve group meetings. The information obtained is not as crisp, sharp and decisive as issue mapping because the data may be skewed and diluted though group interaction. The possibility of testing new, creative positions and "straw" decisions makes focus group research attractive.

Community surveys   These take many forms, from mailers and door-hangers to personal one-on-one interviews. Community surveys can be written or taken verbally, either face-to-face or over the telephone. Response rates are often sketchy when using door-hangers or the U.S. Postal Service for delivery. Lower response percentages can be expected from non-engaged community members and higher responses will come from people who are either for or against some proposed direction, project or decision. Community surveys also tend to strongly reflect recent events that might pertain to questions being raised in the survey.

Each research technique has its strengths and weaknesses, and each can be used in a variety of ways. Detailed information is provided on all three research methods in Chapter 3.

Quantitative vs. Qualitative Research Methods

Quantitative research asks the questions "How many?", "How often?" or even "How strongly?" about a particular subject. The collective response can be assessed in terms of numbers and percentages, and the accuracy determined by confidence levels of "plus or minus" a percentage.

Qualitative research cares less about actual numbers and focuses more on the "whys" and "why nots" of an issue. Putting numbers on qualitative research adds little to the information and may even create confusion.

For instance, a quantitative research report on the same topic might read, "Based on the City's proposal, a survey of 115 neighbors within three blocks of the primary site indicated that 23% opposed the park, 45% supported the park, 17% had no comment, and 15% were classified as damaged ballots. A qualitative research report on the same topic might say, *"As a result of our study, XYZ community generally believes that the new park would be an asset, but significant concerns were raised regarding operating hours and traffic because..."*

Most of the time, public involvement results are based on consensus where generating agreement is preferred to "majority rule." Knowing the root causes of a dispute and understanding the motives behind a particular perception of an issue is generally more important than assessing how many people answer "yes" or "no" to a particular question. The research methods described in Chapter 3 are primarily qualitative.

Stage 3: Strategy Development / Process Design

Strategy development is the act of analyzing research data and early process information to select an overall framework design for the community involvement process. For instance, there would be a significant difference in the process used to manage broad resident involvement arising from a proposal to site a toxic waste processing plant within the borders of a town, than the process of helping a neighborhood come to grips with a group home for disabled senior citizens.

Process design identifies the specific public involvement techniques that might be used in any particular process, and determines how and when to use each of them. Example: If large public events were part of a strategy to gather initial resident input,

Stage 3: Strategy Development/ Process Design

- Develop an overall strategy and design
- Create project objectives and boundaries
- Determine overall approach
- Select tools and techniques

either public hearings, community forums or cable TV call-in shows could do the job. Selecting one or more of these techniques would be part of *process design.*

Design factors that might be considered could include the availability of human resources, the project's budget, gaps in understanding and communicating the issues, and the intensity of conflicts between opposing communities. Other design factors could include points of access provided to participants and stakeholders, and options and alternatives to more traditional methods.

A full discussion of strategy development and process design is included in Chapter 4. A series of charts and forms is included in the appendix to help you in choosing the right strategy, design and tools to get the results you want. The forms highlight the features of strategy development and process design. They explain how each tool and technique might be applied.

Stage 4: Implementation / Action Planning

Project implementation and action planning put into place the community involvement design completed earlier in the process. The goals, objectives, and research findings are used to craft a strategy. That strategy becomes the framework for the process design stage. Community involvement resources, tools and techniques are assembled to form a specific project plan. The implementation stage takes the project plan and generates action. To be effective, stakeholders and participants should be fully engaged by this point to assure support as the plan is being implemented.

Ask and answer the following questions:

1. What specific actions must be taken, and in what order must these actions be taken to achieve the desired outcomes?

2. Who, by name, is responsible for seeing the action is completed?

3. By when will the action be completed?

4. How often will progress be assessed, and how will success be measured?

Upon completion of each activity, project staff must: 1) review and assess performance, 2) adapt to changes, 3) modify the action plan as necessary to keep on track, and 4) redesign the plan which will continue to move, shift and change.

As the plan changes, the reasons should be shared with participants. In this way, the process continues to be honest, open and balanced. Participants can also alert project staff to any unforeseen slips or protocol errors before damage occurs.

Implementation will not always go as planned. Expect that new assessments, modifications, adaptations and redeployment will occur. The questions: "What can be done to make appropriate changes to the design?" and "How will we judge the process and our success at completing the process?" should be asked.

Always do the action plan in writing. Distribute it to people who will help successfully complete the community involvement process. Detailed information on action planning can be found in Chapter 5.

Stage 4: Implementation / Action Planning

- Review process and project objectives
- Identify resources and constraints
- Establish milestones
- Create detailed sequential tasks
- Assign responsibility and performance dates
- Monitor progress and assess performance
- Seek counsel from participants
- Adapt to bumps, barriers and a changing environment

Finally, every action taken during the community involvement implementation process sends a message to those participating. It is important to check frequently with stakeholders to find out:

- What messages are stakeholders and participants hearing?
- Are these the messages we want to send?
- Are the messages accurate?
- Are they timely and helpful?

While implementation of the plan is occurring, project staff must keep in mind the fundamental purpose of the process: To provide accurate, timely and appropriate information to affected interests... and to give everyone access to the discussion who wants a voice. If done properly, the end result of public involvement is better understanding for all stakeholder interests and an opportunity to help the affected public find agreement and direction on a public decision.

Stage 5: Evaluation, Process Review and Capacity Building

At the end of the community involvement process, people who have worked on the project need to gather for a project evaluation. This is a brief (one or two hour) celebration of successes that must include time to ponder the rough spots or failures. The following questions need to be asked during a "project autopsy:"

1. Were the stated outcomes and objectives achieved? If so, why? If not, why not?

2. What parts of the process were technically correct? What went smoothly?

3. What parts of the process that did not go well?

**Stage 5:
Evaluation, Process Review
and Capacity Building**

- Conduct process post mortem

- Document community involvement resources

- Build institutional community-involvement capacity

4. What should be done differently the next time? How could the process be improved?

Based on the information generated during the post mortem, sponsors and managers should create a public involvement standard operating procedure. Participants should not be afraid to criticize any aspect of the process in a helpful and constructive way.

Documentation of the public involvement process is important for building rapport and trust with the broader community. Written policies on public involvement developed with the aid of citizens are becoming standard fare. A list of local community involvement resources should be kept in a central location so others in the agency can tap into them as opportunities arise.

Capacity building within the community is always part of the project agenda. This will allow communities to work together as future issues arise. The need for outside intervention is reduced when communication is improved, understanding is increased, common bonds are built, networks are developed, and leadership is identified and nurtured.

"Civilization is a movement, not a condition; it is a voyage, not a harbor."

—A. Toynbee

Things to Remember

- Give anyone seeing themselves as stakeholders timely, accurate and appropriate information about the issues.

- Give everyone who wants a voice in the process an opportunity to participate.

- By increasing understanding and ownership of a decision, stakeholders will be more likely to support the decision.

- There are five stages in the community involvement process:
  - ○ Stage 1—Pre-Planning
  - ○ Stage 2—Research
  - ○ Stage 3—Strategy Development / Process Design
  - ○ Stage 4—Implementation / Action Planning
  - ○ Stage 5—Evaluation, Process Review and Capacity Building

- Establish clear authority and responsibility for the project.

- Set clear process boundaries and expectations for staff and participants.

- There is a natural resistance to community involvement by internal staff and managers.

- Building community capacity is always part of the job.

- The most difficult part of community involvement is defining issues.

- Conduct the community research and intelligence gathering in advance of a project to avoid unnecessary conflict.

Chapter 3:

Research and Community Information

The Story of Chicken Grove

Harry's staff developed the right facts, figures and perspectives to locate the perfect site for the new fire station. Chicken Grove's Fire Program Planner, Sue Dallas, was assigned the task of developing the project.

Sue wanted to be "hi-tech" in her approach. She found a new graphic information system (GIS) fire station location computer model. After reviewing the experience other towns and cities had already had with the program, she obtained copies of their materials to verify the accuracy. She then fed the population and geographic data into the computer and reviewed the results. Five sites in Chicken Grove met all the modeling constraints.

Sue knew that computer models don't necessarily tell the whole story about site location decisions. So, Sue collected information about the current real estate market and surveyed the business community on how they felt about fire safety issues. Being a good planner, Sue knew that the town's budget was stretched a bit thin trying to keep up with growth, so it was important to keep the capital and operating costs of the new fire station to a minimum.

What's Wrong with Sue's Approach?

Because Sue has helped Harry build fire stations in the past, she was complacent in her search for information. To Sue, research is all about average response times, real estate availability and square footage costs. She assumed that no one would oppose a brand new fire house in their neighborhood. She forgot to assess the social and political environment. Although she did community-based research, Sue and Harry still got a surprise.

Questions to Frame Discussion

- Who are the communities and stakeholders involved in the project?

- What is "at issue"?

- What information is needed?

- What's the best way to obtain this information accurately?

- How will the information be analyzed? How will it be used?

- Can an internal agency research effort generate honest data? If so, how?

Why is Community-Based Research Important?

Public officials make many decisions. Occasionally they may use their common sense or conventional wisdom to make what appears to be a logical decision, but by doing so they set off unanticipated social and political land mines. They blunder into sensitive areas of the community with explosive results. The unintended consequence of their actions can spawn disastrous effects.

Without a full measure of information about an issue or problem it is easy to make mistakes. Often the facts and figures in a project don't tell the whole story. Feelings, beliefs, perceptions and values play a big part in the public's attitude about a public project, issue or problem. Decision makers can't assume what is logical and visible is always what is "at issue." In many cases, what is seen is only a symptom of a much larger irritation.

Community-based research systematically gathers qualitative information from community sources. Once an incident has occurred, a problem is identified or an opportunity realized, community research can help policy makers learn the root causes of the difficulties and understand what irritations are causing (or will cause) an issue to erupt or a dispute to occur. Having this information allows public officials to work toward issue resolution.

Conducting community research in advance also aids in decision making. This advanced research helps most people understand possible community concerns and avoid errors in planning and implementation. Such research can also be effective in anticipating the need for community involvement.

"The effort required to correct an error increases geometrically with time."

—Golub's Law

As noted earlier, research is vital to the community involvement process. Project managers charged with engaging communities and stakeholders need to know when and how to collect community-based information and data, and once gathered what to do with it. Even a limited understanding of community-based research can get the organization started. By following the process, project managers can decide what level of community involvement is necessary and what design components might be effective. They will make better decisions, have an improved chance of resolving issues, and can anticipate future demands. Without the community research, mistakes will be made and issue chaos and conflict will result.

Types of Research

Many good methods exist to collect and analyze community information, but three techniques have repeatedly shown good results when used in a community involvement setting: issue mapping, focus groups and community surveys. The complexity of the issues, and the amount of financial and human resources available will determine which method to apply.

Research Methods:

- Issue Mapping
- Focus Groups
- Community Surveys

Research Features

- Issue mapping provides the most comprehensive information but can be expensive and takes significant time to complete.

- Focus groups use collective interview processes to extract information about critical issues, but need preliminary data as a starting point for discussions.

- Community surveys are simple to develop and apply, but may not provide the depth or breadth of response necessary to make definitive choices.

Issue Mapping

Issue mapping creates a foundation for community-based research and sets the stage for subsequent structured discussions directed at issue resolution. The data may be displayed graphically for visual presentation. Issue mapping provides opportunities for discussions with stakeholders early in the process. It also builds a sense of participant confidence in community involvement.

Interviewees are encouraged to discuss issues, communities and stakeholders' positions on particular matters. Through this conversation they start to vest themselves in the outcome of the community involvement process and in the resolution of problems. By discussing not only their issues but also those of other stakeholder groups, most participants begin to "depolarize" their positions and move toward common interests. Because the interviews are conducted "off-line and without attribution," those interviewed can be candid without fear of embarrassment or reprisals.

Issue mapping is often the first step in stakeholder identification and engagement. It sets the basis for continued discussions and starts bringing stakeholder communities together to resolve issues. A stakeholder's willingness to support the group's decision and work toward broader community support can be a direct result of early inclusion and successful issue mapping.

Issue mapping answers these questions:

1. Who are the people and groups needing a voice in the discussion?

2. What leaders, if any, can play a role in project development?

Issue Mapping Is:

- A series of one-on-one interviews, either face-to-face or on the telephone.

- An analysis of what people say to find out where they agree and disagree, and what they are thinking.

- A report that lists who the key "stakeholders" are for a particular subject and what is "at issue".

- An illustration of typical comments about a topic.

3. What are the stakeholders' issues and how strongly do they embrace their positions on these issues?

4. What, if any, are shared values or common interests?

The Transit Initiative

The Transit Manager asked, "How can community-based research be used to help formulate our proposed mass transit initiative?" This was the first time voters had been asked to fund local mass transit, and it came on the heels of a disastrous regional transit defeat. The answer to her question came in a two-phased response. We would begin with an issue map to collect data from critical stakeholders and communities. It would probably mean conducting extensive face-to-face and telephone interviews, and require significant staff analysis to squeeze all the possible information out of the data. We would follow with collaborative assessment through small group interaction. Researchers would pose optional scenarios to focus groups and determine their reaction to alternatives. "What do you like about this option? What don't you like? How would you change the option to better fit the community's needs?"

Once the research was completed, the City found that of all the potential supporters of a new, independent transit system, single occupancy automobile drivers were the most complimentary and supportive. "How come?" asked the Transit Manager. Even though the focus groups determined that these drivers would never use a bus, they hoped that by putting more busses on the road, other drivers would use mass transit.

Even more important to gaining public support, single occupancy drivers hoped that the bus-bay pull-outs that were included in the proposed initiative, would speed their trips. "No more being stuck behind a smelly bus while it loaded and unloaded passengers." The tax initiative focused on how more busses would reduce congestion and the bus pull-outs were seen as moving more cars, faster. Without community-directed research, the system designers might have missed including a feature that was important to the voting driver.

By the way, the initiative passed by less than 50 votes.

Benefit to the Community Involvement Process

Through issue mapping, the critical factors affecting a problem or project become clearer. Competing stakeholders develop a greater understanding of differing perceptions and values, and may be more likely to search for mutually inclusive alternatives.

The information gathered from an issue map includes perspectives from a broad range of stakeholders and affected groups. They are encouraged to identify every possible issue affecting the discussion. By giving those who have unusually strong feelings a forum to discuss those feelings, a message is sent from the agency that all views are welcome and important to the process. It helps people start to release any pent-up anger, and it sends a message that "your words are important to us." Articulating those strongly held views may generate new discussions and open options that were not considered before by the group. The knowledge gained through issue mapping can also help identify long-term process steps so necessary in getting participants with opposing views to agree.

"If we make peaceful revolution impossible, we make violent revolution inevitable."

John F. Kennedy

The Steps in Issue Mapping

1. Identify information needs

2. Develop the questionnaire and interviewee list

3. Conduct Tier 1 interviews

4. Assemble the stakeholder matrix

5. Conduct Tier 2 interviews

6. Update the stakeholder issue matrix

7. Conduct Tier 3 interviews

8. Summarize the issues

9. Present the information

Steps in Issue Mapping

Step 1 – Identify information needs

The researchers meet with the project sponsors to determine the scope and focus of the inquiry and potential research deliverables.

Step 2 – Develop the questionnaire and interviewee list

Information obtained from project sponsors is used by the researchers to prepare a draft questionnaire and script. After the documents have been prepared, the questionnaire and script are reviewed and approved by the project sponsors, and the materials revised as appropriate.

Step 3 – Conduct first-tier interviews

As a protocol, first-tier interviews are face-to-face. Interviewees should understand the issues in the broadest ways, but have no significant interest in any particular outcome or solution. Examples of first-tier interviewees might include elected officials, agency management, appointed policy-advisors and legislative analysts. They should have a good knowledge of what is at stake and the communities involved in discussions. Tier-one interviewees should not have a predetermined solution in mind. During the first-tier interviews, the names, addresses and phone numbers of people who can speak accurately to the beliefs, feelings and positions of a specific community are collected. The people interviewed should represent a cross section of views within the community.

Tips for Issue Mapping

- Use the telephone to conduct second- and third-tier interviews. This not only saves time, but people will actually discuss issues with more candor and detail.

- Most of the new information received during issue mapping comes from tier-one and tier-two interviews. Tier-three is only needed if conflicting messages and information come during the earlier interview processes.

- People love to be asked for their opinions on controversial topics, and, as a result, become positively engaged in the process.

- Establish interview time limits early in the conversation.

- Helpful suggestions on how issues might be resolved are often found during third-tier interviews.

- Issue mapping is expensive. Cost can be contained by limiting the number of interviews, and by using highly structured survey scripts.

- Absurd or ridiculous polarity quotes ("We need busses running only on one-way streets but 24-hours a day!" or "Busses smell bad so we should get rid of all of them!") can actually be helpful to the process by encouraging moderate voices to state their views.

- Issue mapping is a great way to gradually start bringing polarized communities into the issue resolution process.

- Polarity quotes and statements are provocative and should be directed toward the issues while keeping personal assaults to a minimum.

- Issue map research is qualitative and, by its nature, is difficult to quantify. Be prepared to explain how the data was obtained and how it might best be used.

Tier 1–Elected officials and key staff
Tier 2–High-level leaders
Tier 3–Opinion leaders

First-tier interviewees should have a good understanding of the issue or problem, but should not have a full interest in any particular outcome or solution. Policy makers, city managers, legislators, etc.

Second-tier interviewees are high-level leaders in each of the stakeholder communities, such as executive directors, presidents, or board chairs. They can speak with authority for the groups they represent, but may give two-dimensional "party line" answers.

Third-tier interviewees are opinion leaders. They are the people who grass-roots participants go to when seeking fundamental understanding. They may not speak with formal authority but they have the pulse of the community.

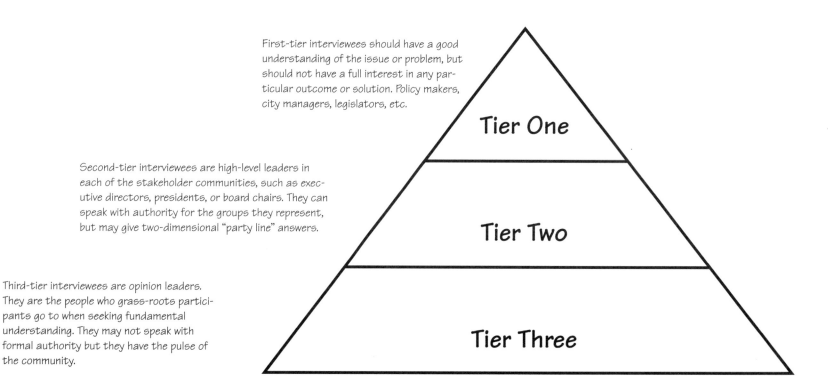

Tier One

Tier Two

Tier Three

Questions asked during a tier-one interview include:

1. What is "at issue?"

2. Who are the communities involved in the discussion?

3. What are their positions on the various issues?

4. Who within those communities can accurately state the community's position?

5. Who are the community's leaders?

A list of potential tier-two interviewees is drawn from this final question. The *Stakeholder Identification List* can be used to record this information. (see Appendix C, page 223)

Step 4 – Assemble the stakeholder matrix

The tier-one data is assembled into a matrix of stakeholders and communities. Factors or features of the problem are listed across the top of the matrix. These features are the ones most frequently mentioned during the interviews. The various stakeholders are listed in the left-hand column. Each cell in the matrix is filled with a particular stakeholder's summary position on each of the features. If opinion polarity exists within a major stakeholder group, and no clear opinion is evident, then an individual issue matrix might be developed just for that community. For example, if the high school students surveyed held multiple, diverse opinions, then a separate issue matrix for high school students could help researchers and sponsors better understand options and alternatives.

Share first-tier research findings with the project sponsors. Determine their reaction to the following questions:

1. What, if anything, was revealed? What is unusual or notable?

2. What stakeholder communities, if any, were missing, not mentioned and/or conspicuously missing?

3. What, if any, anticipated perspectives were not listed as issues?

Step 5 – Conduct second-tier interviews

This group constitutes high-level leaders within stakeholder communities such as homeowners association presidents, Chamber of Commerce executive directors, City department heads, and labor union leaders. They may speak with authority for the group they represent, but may give a two-dimensional "party-line" answer to the questions.

Questions asked during tier-two interviews include:

1. What is your group's position on the issues?

2. Why does your group hold that position?

3. Who or what group might hold a different position than yours?

4. Why might they hold that position?

5. Who else within your community might shed light on the issues?

The questions that should close each tier-two interview are:

6. What communities or perspectives should I be sure to include in our research?

7. Who else might have a stake in this discussion or could represent that community or perspective?

Step 6 – Update the stakeholder issue matrix

The stakeholder issue matrix is updated with fresh information when the second-tier interviews are completed. The names of additional potential interviewees should be added to the *Stakeholder Identification List*. (Appendix C, page 223) This data will be used to plan the tier-three interviews if such interviews are found to be necessary.

Since issue mapping has a relatively high cost to the sponsor, it is important to determine whether a tier-three research effort is needed. In general, if new information is being generated during the tier-two interviews, then proceed to tier-three. If no new information is obtained at tier-two, it is probably unnecessary to go to the time and expense of tier-three interviews.

Step 7 – Conduct third-tier interviews

The third-tier interviews surveys people who are not the formal (institutional) leaders but rather are the groups' opinion leaders. They may not speak with formal authority, but they can read the pulse of the community. For example, every community resources officer in a police department knows who to go to in a neighborhood if they need the "scoop" on who's doing what. Elected officials may have informal policy advisors who are not formal community leaders, but know how the grass-roots voters are leaning.

The critical questions for tier-three interviews are:

1. What is your group's position on the issues?

2. Why does your group hold that position?

3. Who might hold a different position than yours?

4. Why might they hold that position?

5. Are their interests common to all stakeholders?

6. What could people do to resolve the issues that keep them apart?

Again, the questions that should close each interview are:

7. What communities or perspectives should I be sure to include in our research?

8. Who else might have a stake in this discussion or could represent that community or perspective?

Step 8 – Issue Summary

Information gathered from charts, tables, notes, and from the stakeholder issue matrices are used to summarize the interview findings. The researcher's first job is to highlight the points on which everyone agreed as a starting position for discussion. These points of agreement establish common ground for all participants. Common ground is sometimes difficult to find, and diligence is the key to locating it.

Next, important issues for which there is general but not unanimous agreement must be determined. Subtle points of disagreement should be highlighted and any suggestions of resolution posed by the interviewees noted.

Finally, strong disagreement and polarity should be identified. For each polarity statement made by one community, a balancing polarity statement on the other side needs to be constructed. Direct quotes or "typical statements" illustrating the extremes of the dispute can be a cathartic device during a group discussion. The more extreme the illustration, the better it is for creating clear choices. The opposite sides of the poles are placed side-by-side in the written report for all to see. Any suggestions for issue resolution will also be stated in the report.

Step 9 – Present the information

The issue summary presented to the project staff and their reaction, should be recorded. Their input can be used to correct errors or suggest ways to improve the report.

Focus Groups

Focus groups for community-based research differ from those used by private market research firms to test public reaction to products and services. Both types of focus groups use collective interviewing, group moderators and detailed recording procedures in order to keep the discussion on track and focused. Both create a series of questions prepared and tested in advance to gauge a visceral reaction to an issue or product.

Community-directed focus groups have one distinct difference in that they are not benign observers or consumers. Participants may also be key stakeholders in substantive discussions to find solutions to problems, define policies and develop projects. The process is designed and participants selected to assure disagreement

Community-directed focus groups can:

- Determine perceptions, feelings, beliefs, attitudes and expectations.

- Capture scenarios and examples to use as subsequent illustrations.

- Diagnose problems and identify opportunities.

- Build a sense of community.

- Establish a sense of direction.

- Foster new ideas.

- Produce data quickly and easily at low cost.

- Encourage broad involvement of the community.

- Include users of the data in the sample.

- Generate optional resolutions.

Community-directed focus groups require:

- Extensive advance preparation.

- Careful stakeholder and community sampling.

- Experienced and highly skilled moderators and documenters.

- Time to find, attract, schedule and engage participants.

- Multiple group sessions to ensure quality sampling.

Participant difficulties can include...

- Domination by one or two people with strong substantive feelings.

- Intense, non-topical interpersonal emotions.

- Generalized concerns that do not relate to the focus topic.

and polarity, but as they share ideas, values and beliefs, researchers want to see how their opinions and positions on the target topic change. Throughout the discussion participants become better informed. Researchers ask, "What critical words and concepts seemed to enhance their understanding and movement?" Since well-designed focus groups are safe places to discuss feelings, information flows freely.

Features of Focus Groups

Focus groups are great ways to collect large amounts of qualitative data in relatively short amounts of time. They may be used to bring critical stakeholders into the planning process, and begin building trust within and between communities. Focus groups may also be used in conjunction with issue maps and community surveys to test initial research findings.

Typical focus group sessions have between 8 and 15 participants, are conducted by experienced moderators and last from 90 to120 minutes. Participants are selected based on perspective, affiliation, or demographic characteristics. An interview format is used to assure a safe, informal environment.

Successful Focus Groups

Using focus groups as the only research method to study issues may not provide sufficient understanding of potential decisions, policies and projects, but if used in combination with other techniques focus groups can:

- Confirm or contradict other research.
- Provide greater depth and breadth of knowledge.
- Develop substantive options and alternatives.
- Start the issue resolution process.

An additional benefit to focus groups is an understanding of "why" people feel the way they do.

The following is a step-by-step process for conducting focus groups.

Step 1: Participants

Focus-group participants are generally hand-picked based on their anticipated perspective or their status in a key stakeholder community. It is important that participants understand the nature of the issues being tested and the objectives desired from the research.

Demographic factors such as job level, education, occupation, race, culture, gender, and age may be important selectives for participants. *Homogeneous focus groups* consist of people who share a selective while *heterogeneous focus groups* strive for diversity. Researchers assemble homogeneous groups to test the internal consistency of data coming from a particular community or demographic selective, while heterogeneous groups are used to assess how different communities interact with each other when faced with a particular topic.

Conducting Focus Groups:

1. Select participants

2. Select moderator

3. Decide meeting logistics

4. Develop research questions

5. Greet participants prior to the session

6. Conduct the session

7. Analyze the data

Try to identify twice as many participants as are actually needed. Scheduling times mutually agreeable for the meetings is difficult.

Step 2: The Moderator

An experienced moderator who does not have a stake in the project or topic should be selected to manage the research sessions. A professional moderator may be found by calling local universities, market research firms, or through referrals.

The moderator should be absolutely clear as to expected process outcomes from the sessions, and the research methodology used. Let the moderator help you develop the actual questions and meeting process.

Step 3: Meeting Logistics

Meeting planning can make or break a focus group. Pay attention to details such as:

- Room size and seating arrangement.

- Location.

- Physical environmental factors, i.e., windows, lighting, air circulation, heating/cooling, and accessories.

- Incompatible environmental distractions like noise or odors. Serve appropriate food and beverages. Coffee and muffins work for morning meetings. Soft drinks and cookies are good for afternoon sessions. Serve a light dinner for evening events.

Successful focus group moderators:

- Encourage group discussions.

- Manage the group's resources, time, group dynamics, and behavior.

- Guide the discussion without contributing to or directing it.

- Actively listen and ask questions.

- Develop rapport with the group.

- Pull facts and data from the group.

- Remain neutral and unbiased.

- Help the group come to closure.

Scheduling focus group sessions is difficult. Decide how many unique focus group sessions are needed to accomplish the research objectives, and make sure to invite sufficient participants to fill all the sessions. It may be advisable to hold a series of focus groups with different participants to gain an initial understanding of the topic. If needed, hold subsequent sessions to test and confirm earlier results. As a rule, identify twice as many potential participants as are actually needed to fill the sessions.

Distribute invitations in phases so as to control booking. An initial telephone call to determine interest can save time, but then send personalized invitations to each participant signed by someone they know, respect or admire. As the host of a focus group make sure you have token appreciation gifts available for participants. Take the time to say "thank you" when the session is over. Community-directed focus groups rarely (if ever) pay participants for their time. They may ask about compensation when you contact them, so be prepared to address the volunteer nature of the contribution.

When scheduling focus groups, consider...

- The participants' schedules and their ability to attend the session.
- The time of day, week, month and year.
- If sessions may conflict with religious holidays or community events.
- A location that is easy to find and accessible to people with disabilities.
- Parking convenience and public transportation.

Body Language

Remain seated if you're not leading the group. To get the group's attention and assume leadership, stand up. Negotiate this convention with your co-facilitators and sponsors in advance of a meeting.

There are many ways to set up the room for a focus group, but one of the most effective is an "Open-U" with participants seated around the outside and the facilitator at the open end. The entrance to the room should always be behind and out of the direct line-of-sight of the participants. A name tent should be prepared for each participant so the moderator can call participants by their first names, if appropriate.

Seating participants can be a concern. One option is to just allow people to sit where they want with no consideration for personal interaction or philosophic bent. On the other hand, if personal interaction may hinder the group's performance, determine who should sit where, organize the name tents and anticipate location.

Documenting and recording the data generated from a focus group session needs planning, too. Several methods are available, and each has strengths and weaknesses. A person taking notes, either by hand, using a laptop computer or a court reporter device, is one method. Another way is to use a central sound recording system. Some private market research firms use one-way mirrors to videotape sessions. Whatever method is used, participants should be informed at the beginning of the focus group exactly how the session will be documented.

Step 4: Research Questions

Because focus group questions are difficult to develop, try to find research professionals to lend support. Many universities and colleges teach classes in research methods. Their students can be wonderful volunteer resources. The student gains practical experience and the agency gets professional help at little or no cost.

Work with the project sponsor to develop a framework agenda. The objectives of the research need to be examined to determine what information can be obtained. A few "off-the-cuff" questions can be initially developed to get started.

The following questions need to be asked when designing focus groups:

1. What do we hope to achieve from the session?

2. What do we want to learn?

3. How will the data be collected?

4. How will the data be turned into usable information?

5. What are the discussion boundaries?

Once the baseline questions are clearly developed, it is important to determine how much more detail is necessary. The project sponsors and researchers should work with the moderator to refine the subordinate questions. Questions should be open-ended and provocative to encourage discussion while keeping the group clearly on point.

A dry run using a limited number of process participants and some of the project staff members should be conducted. At the conclusion of the dry run, the participants should be asked to list any questions that were confusing or difficult to answer. Questions can then be revised based on the initial participant reaction and comments.

Step 5: Greet Participants Prior to the Session

Greet participants as they arrive to make them feel comfortable. Show them to the meeting room and indicate where restrooms and refreshments are located. Assess their "temperature" before the focus group begins. It is usually helpful to engage them in light conversation ("How was your day?" "How 'bout those Mets?" "Did you have trouble finding the meeting location or a parking place?").

Step 6: Conduct the Session

If an agency representative is available and willing, have them open the focus group with a brief welcome and an introduction to the topic. The moderator will normally have participants introduce themselves to each other, review the agenda, and give instructions about how the session will be managed.

Use an easy ice breaker question to send the message to the group that it is safe to participate. This icebreaker may or may not be associated with the topic of the focus group. When the group is ready, the moderator moves to the prepared script and questions.

More detailed instruction for actually conducting focus group meetings is contained in *Chapter 6: Meetings and Their Role in Community Involvement.*

Flaming Comments

At the end of a focus group session, some moderators ask for any additional input that participants want to give that was not part of the prepared agenda. Know as "flaming comments" because of their provocative content, these comments provide participants with an outlet for issues they really wanted to discuss but didn't. A risky practice, but if handled properly flaming comments can provide an important context for the sponsors and the researchers.

Step 7: Analyze the Data

Toward the end of a community-directed focus group session, ask participants to confirm their understanding of the topic, identify issues that they agree on, prioritize their feelings, and summarize what they heard the group say. When reviewing discussion notes, identify particular points of strong polarity and topics of almost unanimous agreement.

Complete a summary report for each focus group. If there are multiple sessions, consolidate the individual reports into a master summary. Note how different groups approached the topic. Identify situations where participant demographics and composition may have caused an aberration in the results. Debrief staff observers to get their impressions of the session. Present the final research report to the project sponsors for their interpretation of the findings. It may be helpful to actually present an executive summary of the research to participants in the community involvement process as a starting point for their discussions.

Other difficulties with focus groups might include:

- Inexperienced moderators and recorders.

- Loss of control during the meeting can turn a congenial discussion into an angry forum.

- People with strong personal feelings may misuse the group's time.

- Participants are sometimes hard to find, attract, select, and engage.

- Representatives of various stakeholder communities may be difficult to locate.

- Interpersonal conflicts may arise between participants.

Community Surveys

Community surveys can provide an inexpensive way to obtain large amounts of broad-based data. They can take the form of written "check-the-box" forms received by mail, face-to-face intercepts at shopping malls, or even the unwelcome telephone calls received just as dinner is being served. They can ask questions as specific as "what time does the water meter reader usually visit your home" to something as generalized as "how well do you think your elected officials are doing?" They can examine generalized resident perceptions on a variety of topics simultaneously, and they provide the most help for community-directed research when used in conjunction with other research techniques.

Unfortunately, when agencies try to use stand-alone community surveys to drive decision making by policy makers, they attempt to quantify data that is fundamentally qualitative. A report goes to the city council stating that, "58 percent of the residents of ABC neighborhood believe that additional police protection is needed." That statement, by itself, should raise more questions than answers. Using percentages to reflect feelings and perceptions gives the typical reader an inflated sense of confidence in the research. All that can be concluded from the statement is that on a particular day of the week and month, a particular, limited and often self-selected population sample of a geographic region checked a particular box on a particular questionnaire about public safety that they interpreted in a particular way. Without seeing the question and how it was worded, and without knowing how the survey instrument was developed and applied, the statement is of little value to the decision-maker.

Survey instruments may give as much information as they gather, and can stimulate community conversations on specific topics. Surveys may also help focus information obtained from other types of research. They can gauge reaction to potential public decisions or resolutions to problems. "If the choice was either to do A or to do B, which would you prefer?"

Community surveys can be widely distributed at a relatively low cost. Well-crafted, professionally constructed survey instruments applied to a large sample may point to areas of further research, and telephone surveys can quickly document public reaction to immediate issues.

Agencies using community surveys may have difficulties managing the research process. Because they are so easy, quick and inexpensive to develop and distribute, community survey instruments are often hastily prepared by project staff with no training or practical experience in research methods. The participants in community surveys may be required to interpret the questions, so the possible range of interpretations leads to widely varying responses. Results can be skewed toward a "favorable" or predetermined response. Historically, written mail-out or door-hanger type surveys have low response rates, and the people responding to such surveys may be self-selected as members of polarized communities. People holding moderate views on a topic may not feel an urgency to return the instrument.

Fundamental Survey Questions

Before designing any kind of a community survey process, the following questions need to be asked and answered by project sponsors:

1. What do we hope to learn?

2. What type of data will we collect?

3. What methods will we use?

4. How will the results be analyzed and used?

5. Who do we want to sample and how large is the sample?

6. What response rate do we hope to achieve?

7. How will participants be found and engaged?

8. What are the costs?

9. Is timing important to the results?

10. How will we use the results?

Step 1: Pre-survey preparation

The agency sponsors must clearly highlight their expectations to the researcher, the purpose of the study, deliverables that are expected, the resources available to complete work, and the constraints to research which may create difficulties. Fundamentally, sponsors should answer the question, "What are the key issues and driving questions on which we want citizens to comment?"

Participants interact in two basic ways, remotely or interpersonally, with surveys. Within these two ways are many different survey techniques and a range of other choices that project staff must make before initiating research.

Remote surveys include any technique that avoids personal contact during the question and answer period. Written surveys completed privately by the respondent, Internet surveys, and automated telephone surveys all fall into this category. Questions must be precise and clear enough to allow respondents to accurately interpret each question and make a considered response. Remote surveys require great skill and testing of questions prior to administration.

Personal surveys involve a surveyor and a respondent. The surveyor either directly asks the question or is available to the participant to clarify questions about the instrument. Face-to-face directed conversations, personal telephone surveys, and intercept surveys fall into this category. A skilled interviewer may further hone a range of responses, and subordinate or clarifying questions can be raised to gain a better understanding of the response.

Steps in Community Surveys:

1. Pre-survey preparation

2. Design the questionnaire

3. Pretest the instrument

4. Distribution of the survey

5. Analysis

Open-ended vs Close-ended Questions

Designing the questions is the most important part of developing a questionnaire. Open-ended questions allow participants to craft their own responses in their own words, and generate a more precise response. Close-ended or limited-response questions provide easier data tabulation but by asking participants to select from a series of pre-identified choices, new thoughts, ideas, emerging issues, or unique solutions may not flow forward.

For issue identification and resolution, use open-ended questions whenever the sample size will allow. Close-ended questions are typically used to rate service or alternatives from a limited universe of possibilities. If members of the community have limited language skills, close-ended questions may be more inclusive.

Types of Responses

Another choice that must be made in advance of designing and administering a community survey is the type of response that is desired. Are we looking for a generalized community opinion, or something precisely targeted to an issue or an event? Do we desire thoughtful contemplation or an immediate visceral reaction unaffected by survey marketing or education? Survey questions may be created to solicit either close-ended or open-ended responses; each has advantages and disadvantages.

Close-ended responses might include "yes" or "no," "true" or "false," "A, B or C" multiple choice, or even a continuum of concrete responses. Large sample surveys are easiest to administer with close-ended questions where there are a limited number of responses and when they are printed on computer scanning sheets with optical readers processing the data. Open-ended questions allow respondents wider latitude in their answers. Smaller sample-sized surveys with targeted open-ended questions provide a richer, deeper set of responses to the researcher, but require a more deliberate analysis process.

Survey Administration Support

There are several options an agency might choose for developing and administering a community survey. One of the potentially easiest methods is to simply hire a professional market research firm to do the job. Agency experiences vary, but a good, professional research firm can march sponsors through the survey process in a quality way from start to finish. Sponsors still need to take time to guide research decisions and clearly state what information is desired when the project is completed. Unfortunately, the cost of hiring a professional firm is often more than agency staff can afford.

College and university faculties can be very helpful in supporting local government research. They may have students who need real-world encounters and who would willingly volunteer their time in exchange for the experience. As with any decision on research, quality should be a concern. Agencies should make sure student researchers are working with, and under the direct supervision of, experienced faculty. Availability of resources from colleges and universities may be dependent upon the academic calendar and personal timing. If an agency is willing to work with such restrictions, it can get good results at relatively low cost using university students.

Community volunteers are also an option to supplement professional resources. They can bring energy, enthusiasm and resources to a research project, but need professional supervision, direction and support. For instance, creating the survey instrument would not be an area of assignment for typical community volunteers, but perhaps administering the instrument, door-to-door, to community residents is.

Finally, project staff are the usual resources tapped by agencies to undertake community survey research. Their availability is clearly a plus, but they normally lack experience in survey design and training in survey administration and analysis. Likewise, staff may bring a predisposition or bias to the research responses that could be reflected in the findings. Even if staff are absolutely balanced in their approach and develop excellent survey tools, their employment and status on the project make them suspect by stakeholders.

Open-ended Questions:

1. Allow participants to craft their own responses in their own words.

2. Generate a more precise response.

3. Encourage new thoughts, ideas, emerging issues or unique solutions.

4. Work best with small sample sizes.

5. Encourage issue identification and resolution.

6. Require more time to code, summarize and process.

7. Promote richer analysis and more subtleties.

Step 2: Design the questionnaire

Developing the questions is the most difficult and time-consuming part of the survey process. The question designer must understand the context and boundaries of the research, so a meeting with project sponsors to review draft questions is necessary. Instrument design is a creative process, so several iterations may be required.

Questions should be clear to the reader. If one hundred people read the question, they should all interpret it the same way. Here are a few ideas to keep in mind when designing a survey questionnaire:

- Avoid words that may have different meanings. For instance, the term *"one year"* could mean the previous calendar year or the past twelve months.

- Double-barreled questions often group several items and ask for only one response to the question. For example, "How important are the neighborhood block watch, community police, and graffiti programs in your community? Very, Somewhat or Not at all." A respondent may think the block watch is very important but think the graffiti program is not. The question, however, allows only one response.

- Leading questions and steering the respondent toward a predetermined response should be avoided. Leading questions also make the instrument suspect and cloud the research results.

- Questions surveying participant demographics can be very helpful and should be included if responses may vary depending on age, income, ethnicity and/or gender. An option allowing the participants not to complete the demographic questions should also be provided.

- Participants will be more prone to responding to demographic questions if they are asked toward the end of the survey rather than at the beginning. First, they will understand and trust the survey purpose by that time. Second, they will have invested their time in answering the major portion of the survey, and feel a need for completion.

- Keep the questionnaire as short and simple as possible. Fewer people will complete and return a survey that is longer and difficult to answer.

- If a large sample size is anticipated, limit the number of questions using an open-ended format.

- Assure legibility by using appropriate fonts and sizes.

- If the survey is mailed with a postage paid reply, design the instrument to be folded and easily inserted into the reply envelope.

Distribution Design

Decisions on how the actual survey will be taken should be made prior to survey design. A survey that is to be mailed to 2000 residences within a ten square block area will take on a very different look than a telephone survey of 800 randomly selected local telephone numbers.

Direct mail is very popular because it has a relatively low cost per questionnaire distributed. Such surveys can be assembled quickly, and may be conducted annually if a long-term trend analysis is sought. Large sample surveys generally take the

Close-Ended or Limited Response Questions:

1. Select from a series of pre-identified choices.

2. Work well for generating responses from large population samples.

3. Are useful for general service rating.

4. Prioritize alternatives from a limited universe of possibilities.

5. Require more data tabulation using easier, simpler technology.

6. Are more inclusive when participants have limited language skills.

Methods for Survey Distribution

- Direct mail
- Newspaper inserts
- Utility bill inserts
- Door hangers
- Telephone interviews
- Intercept surveys
- Personal face-to-face interviews
- The Internet

direct mail route. More care must be taken in preparing the questions to avoid misunderstanding or confusion. Since it is a written instrument, participants must be literate or accommodation should be provided for those who cannot read. If the area being surveyed has multiple ethnic populations, versions of the questionnaire should be available in all prevalent languages and in Braille. Direct mail has traditionally had low response rates. To increase response, use self-mailers or prepaid self-addressed envelopes.

Other techniques similar to direct mail include newspaper and utility bill inserts. Unit costs are low but response rates are also low.

Hand delivered "door hangers" are less expensive to deliver and have features similar to direct mail. If the delivery person makes a personal contact with the potential participant, experience has shown a slightly higher response rate. If a follow-up and personal survey pick-up is included in the door hanger service, response rates can again increase.

Telephone interviews are a staple of local government for longitudinal citizen satisfaction surveys. A survey team of paid telephone solicitors are given randomly selected local phone numbers. They pick a time period and "dial and smile." Sample sizes are smaller and response rates are higher than with direct mail, but since this is an interview process the scripts being used must be carefully prepared to avoid misunderstandings. Distribution costs per survey unit are generally higher but questions can be more precisely targeted to the sponsor's research needs.

Intercept surveys and personal face-to-face interviews take parts of the written survey process (direct mail) and the telephone interview process, in an attempt to increase sample size, increase response rates and manage costs. Intercept surveys are effective ways of capturing large sample sizes where many people are gathered together for a period of time. Airport and bus terminals, athletic events, concerts, shopping malls and conventions are good venues for intercept surveys. For smaller sample sizes personal appointments and door-to-door interviews can work. The response rates are much higher than for direct mail, and if researchers want to "drill down" into the data, the people conducting the interview can ask further probing questions.

The Internet is now available to change the face of community-directed research. More and more people are joining the Web, so electronic surveys are becoming popular. As with all surveys, the quality and size of the sample should be a concern. Self-selection is probably even more of a problem with electronic surveys, since there are specific demographics that emerge as being more computer literate, and others who have little or no access to computer technology.

Here are some things to consider when selecting a distribution model:

- Before determining how to distribute the survey, determine who will be asked to complete the survey and tailor the process to their needs.

- Do most of the potential respondents have telephones? If so, consider the efficiency of telephone interviews. If not, a telephone interview is not a choice.

- How many people will be surveyed? If the participants live in a small area, it may be cost effective to have nonprofit, civic or youth groups deliver the surveys door-to-door and in the process, earn some extra money for their organizations.

- What is the budget? If the sample group is large, the total cost of printing and direct mail can be expensive.

- Is the community geographically close? If so, door-to-door interviews may be best.

- Do the questionnaires need to be provided in alternative formats including large print, Braille, audiotape, or in a foreign language? Local libraries will usually translate the documents into Braille.

- When translating into another language, it is best to use someone from the community to ensure the correct dialect.

Step 3: Pre-Test the Instrument

Pre-test the questionnaire using project sponsors and staff members who are not involved in the project, and track the length of time it takes to complete it. Determine if the time needed to fill out the survey will encourage people to respond or will discourage participation. Identify questions that are confusing and rewrite them for clarity. Finally, make sure that the sequencing of questions (flow) is appropriate to the research purpose.

Ask, "Are the test questions we're asking the ones in which we want to invest our limited time and money?"

If not, rewrite the questions and re-test the survey until the instrument is as good as possible.

Step 4: Distribute Survey

Select a period of time for survey administration. Let everyone involved know the survey is going out. Inform the public information officer for the agency since there will be calls asking, "Hey, what is this?" If the agency responsible for the research has elected officials, let them know, too. It might be appropriate to send a news release to the local papers, radio and TV stations that people will be receiving a questionnaire.

Some additional tips for survey administration include:

- Plan a date for survey distribution that gives the researchers a little extra time. Something always seems to go wrong. Printing equipment malfunctions, the interviewer's child gets sick, the weather turns bad, and there's a misspelled word on page four that has to be changed.

- If hiring a professional public research firm, check their credentials and references.

- If the community has a radio station that reads the newspaper, books and other materials for blind residents, they may be willing to read the survey materials over the air and allow listeners to call in with their responses. They may also provide audiotapes for distribution.

- Bulk mail saves money, but delivery is delayed; build delays into the schedule.

- Set a cut-off date to have all surveys submitted and stick to that date.

- Start entering the data into the computers as soon as possible to anticipate a last minute surge of responses.

Step 5: Analysis of the Survey

Everything has been submitted from the field surveyors. The sample size is adequate. The data has been entered into the database.

Document the original survey design, and determine what variations may have occurred during the actual survey process. Were there questions in the survey instrument that did not prove to be helpful? Was there confusion on the part of survey workers? How many actual responses were received? What was the response rate? Compare the number of actual samples received to the desired response. Prepare a report reflecting how well the research process was completed and how well it was received by the community.

Review the raw data. Are their clear trends emerging? Was polarity in responses evident? Did participants respond to the questions in ways that could give your sponsors additional information above and beyond that expected?

Take a first cut at identifying common themes and messages in the data. Remember that it is more important to identify common issues and perceptions than to calculate sampling errors and statistical significance. Attempting to quantify fundamentally qualitative data gives a false sense of confidence in the data, and can cloud the important qualitative data that comes from the research.

Things to Remember about Research

- Save time, money, trouble and avoid false starts by always doing research in advance of project planning.

- Review the draft framework strategy and overall design for community research before proceeding.

- Look to "friendly faces" to start the research, but continue to seek people who might suggest a different approach or have strong opinions regarding the issues.

- Always include people in the research might have a significant effect on any suggested solutions.

Chapter 4:
Strategy Development and Process Design

The Story of Chicken Grove

Chief Harry and Planner Sue knew how to design and manage a community involvement process. It was not only outlined in state law but also in local ordinance. They'd successfully completed four other fire stations over the past ten years using the same model.

The Mayor and Council were expecting a "blue-ribbon" citizens group to review the proposal, so one was created. The Fire Department would hold a meeting of the Citizens Review Committee to discuss the proposal. By the end of that meeting the group would hold a public hearing on the matter. If anyone came to the meeting or the public hearing, they could speak.

After the Committee endorsed staff's recommendations, the project would be placed on the next available Town Council agenda. Planner Sue would have the architect do some renderings for the press. These drawings would be part of the Council presentation. The Council would approve construction and thank Fire Department staff and the Citizens Review Committee for their hard work.

Construction would start on the new fire station in about 90 days.

What's wrong?

Nothing yet. Everything seems to be going well with the strategy and process Sue and Harry developed. It was just like the process they used in the four previous fire stations projects. It had worked before. But things were different now, and Harry and Sue were complacent. They believed that because the strategy had worked in the past, it would work again. "After all," Chief Harry said later, "how many times do you have to build a fire station before you get it right???"

Harry and Sue were about to learn that their strategy was wrong! So their process design was wrong.

Questions to Frame the Discussion

- What is the desired outcome of the community involvement process?
- What are the process objectives that, if completed, will achieve the desired outcome?
- What tools and techniques can be used to support the process objectives?
- If the action plan is implemented and completed, are these collective actions sufficient to assure success?

Deciding to Continue with a Community Involvement Effort

After completing the initial community-directed research, the agency staff and sponsor must decide whether community involvement is appropriate and can be helpful in resolving the current public questions and/or controversy. Use the following chart to assess the environment and make a decision on whether to proceed:

Questions to determine if community involvement can be helpful	Yes	No	Maybe
Do the stakeholder communities feel sufficient pressure to get them to the table and engage in open discussions?			
Are the leaders within these communities personally committed to resolving the issues?			
Are there valid concerns that need to be addressed? If yes, can they be resolved?			
Are the issues at stake sufficient to warrant the time and effort it takes to find agreement?			
Are there enough resources to complete the process?			
Are there any fatal flaws that would keep a community involvement process from being successful?			

There are legitimate reasons for delaying or avoiding public involvement. Sometimes the various communities are too splintered to come together and resolve common problems without significant preparation in advance of engagement. Other times, the political environment will not allow a resolution process to take place. Demographic and economic factors within a community can work against short-term issue resolution and affect the types of community involvement that can be helpful. Occasionally, it's just not the right time to have this talk. If any of these conditions exist, consider delaying initiation of public involvement activities.

If conditions are ripe for community discussions, then move forward to develop a strategy and design a public involvement process.

Strategy Development and Process Design

Strategy development is the act of analyzing research data and earlier draft design information, and selecting an overall framework for the community involvement process. Simply stated, there are numerous social, educational, economic and demographic factors that have an effect on a public decision. When analyzed, these factors can help agency staff determine what specific processes might best be used to launch a community discussion.

"You don't have to explain something you never said"

—Calvin Coolidge

Tips for Strategy Development and Process Design

- Develop a framework strategy.
- Create project objectives, limitations and boundaries.
- Determine an overall approach.
- Select tools and techniques.

Process design applies specific community involvement tools and techniques to the strategy once it has been developed.

Process design factors

- Availability of human resources.

- The project's budget.

- Gaps in understanding and communicating the issues.

- Intensity of conflicts between opposing communities.

- Points of access.

- Options and alternatives to the more traditional community involvement methods.

A statement of *strategy development* might be, "Create a seven-person citizen board to collect and analyze community input, and present recommendations to the City Council." Statements that might appear in a *process design* could include, "Schedule and complete three community forums to discuss XYZ over the next six weeks" or "hold one cable TV call-in show, three civic club speaker's bureau presentations, and two public hearings to gather broad initial citizen input." Selecting the specific tools and techniques to accomplish the strategy is part of *process design*.

Appendices A and B are tables listing Meeting Techniques and Communication Tools useful in public involvement. These charts reference information needed for designing both strategies and processes. They highlight the features of the techniques, explain generally how to use them, and suggest situations in which a technique might be best applied.

What strategies and designs would you use?

What factors would you use in creating a public involvement strategy? How about selecting the tools and techniques to help you engage the community? Take a look at the following situations that might require some very different approaches to public involvement. How would your approach differ in each circumstance?

A group home for disabled senior citizens is planned for a new residential subdivision.	VERSUS	A toxic waste processing plant is proposed for an existing industrial area.
Comment on broad revisions to a twenty-year general land use plan.	VERSUS	Public comment on a new Wal-Mart store planned for the corner of Oak and 3rd Street.
Informing community members about a change in the police department's "hot pursuit" policies.	VERSUS	Police management asking residents to help develop, recommend and decide on the department's "hot pursuit" policies.

Assessing the Research and Environmental Factors

Consider the following internal questions:

- What can the agency do to develop alternatives?
- What time limits are being imposed on the process?
- What resources are available to undertake the work?
- What barriers to public involvement exist?

Create Project Objectives and Boundaries

It helps to know your limits, boundaries and level of authority as you move forward. As you develop your strategy and design the methods for accomplishing your goals, seek clear direction from the community-directed research completed in initiating the project. Show the results of the research to your sponsor and to the leadership of the communities involved. Ask them what they believe is necessary. Request their assessment of how reasonable expectations might be established. What are their objectives? What do they hope to achieve as a result of their investment of their time, their talent, the scarce resources that could be placed in other opportunities, and the political capital it will cost all parties?

Collect and record their responses. Construct a one-page summary of what you believe the project goals and objectives might be, list the goals under a corresponding heading, likewise objectives, the boundaries that clearly delineate the limits of the discussion, and the resources that will be used.

Can a public involvement process be effective?

Using research data, answer the following questions:

- What is at issue?
- Are the issues salient?
- What communities are involved?
- Have the communities become polarized in their positions?
- What is the level of polarity?
- Have leaders emerged to help organize their communities? If so, do they recognize each other as legitimate stakeholders?
- Are the leaders willing to enter into discussions?
- Is there any movement within leadership to find common interests?
- Has a range of alternatives been identified?
- Are the alternatives tractable?

As a courtesy, honor your sponsor by discussing this initial planning piece prior to distributing to community leaders. Make adjustments as needed, then negotiate these goals, objectives, limits, boundaries and resources with the leaders of the stakeholder communities potentially participating in the process. Put it in writing, get it signed if possible, and keep it always in front of the participants as you work through issues. This establishes your charter for the period of time you're together.

Developing a Strategy and Process Design that Fits the Situation

Strategies for formal processes generally require greater planning and more resources. When the issues are more polarized and intense, the numbers of community groups and actual participants greater, the economic, political and social stakes higher, then you could expect a more formal public involvement process being needed. Part of your strategy might be to increase the amount of research and provide more information to a broader segment of stakeholders. The intensity and formality of communication could increase, and there would be greater potential for snipers and the media to broaden the discussion, bringing collateral issues into the debate.

Projects with fewer stakeholder communities and participants might require less formal community involvement strategies. When a controversy has a limited geographic interest or is isolated to just a few stakeholders, meetings might be more limited.

Caution: Never underestimate the power of a determined stakeholder, sniper or the media to "grow" the controversy.

Any of the examples of public issues illustrated in the charts contained in this chapter could expand to monumental size...or shrink into a simple, civil discussion. Each situation is unique. The scope and magnitude of discussions often depend on how the leaders of the communities at odds with one another perceive the stakes and what is at issue.

Take a look at the situations described in the tables that follow. For each factor indicate how the issue described in the heading might rate in your community. Use the scale of "formal to informal" shown on the next page.

Rating Scale for Formal to Informal

Formal Process	Community Involvement Feature	Informal Process
Broad	Level of community interest	Narrow
High	Community history and profile	Low
High	Saliency of subject	Low
Many	Number of stakeholder communities	Few
High	Issue polarity/intensity	Low
High	Potential for political interest/impact	Low
High	Potential for media coverage	Low
High	Needed/desired number of participants	Low
High	Anticipated number of participants	Low
High	Individual and/or collective leadership within stakeholder groups	Low
High	Potential for economic gain or loss	Low
High	Potential for community impact/change	Low
High	Potential for social power gain or loss	Low

A group home for disabled senior citizens is planned for a new residential subdivision.		A toxic waste processing plant is proposed for an existing industrial area.	
	Level of community interest		Level of community interest
	Community history and profile		Community history and profile
	Saliency of subject		Saliency of subject
	Number of stakeholder communities		Number of stakeholder communities
	Issue polarity/intensity		Issue polarity/intensity
	Potential for political interest/impact		Potential for political interest/impact
	Potential for media coverage		Potential for media coverage
	Needed/desired number of participants		Needed/desired number of participants
	Anticipated number of participants		Anticipated number of participants
	Individual and/or collective leadership within stakeholder groups		Individual and/or collective leadership within stakeholder groups
	Potential for economic gain or loss		Potential for economic gain or loss
	Potential for community impact/change		Potential for community impact/change
	Potential for social power gain or loss		Potential for social power gain or loss

Comment on broad revisions to a twenty-year general land use plan		Public comment on a new Wal-Mart store planned for the corner of Oak and 3rd Street	
	Level of community interest		Level of community interest
	Community history and profile		Community history and profile
	Saliency of subject		Saliency of subject
	Number of stakeholder communities		Number of stakeholder communities
	Issue polarity/intensity		Issue polarity/intensity
	Potential for political interest/impact		Potential for political interest/impact
	Potential for media coverage		Potential for media coverage
	Needed/desired number of participants		Needed/desired number of participants
	Anticipated number of participants		Anticipated number of participants
	Individual and/or collective leadership within stakeholder groups		Individual and/or collective leadership within stakeholder groups
	Potential for economic gain or loss		Potential for economic gain or loss
	Potential for community impact/change		Potential for community impact/change
	Potential for social power gain or loss		Potential for social power gain or loss

Informing community members about a change in the police department's "hot pursuit" policies		Police management asking residents to help develop, recommend and decide on the department's "hot pursuit" policies	
	Level of community interest		Level of community interest
	Community history and profile		Community history and profile
	Saliency of subject		Saliency of subject
	Number of stakeholder communities		Number of stakeholder communities
	Issue polarity/intensity		Issue polarity/intensity
	Potential for political interest/impact		Potential for political interest/impact
	Potential for media coverage		Potential for media coverage
	Needed/desired number of participants		Needed/desired number of participants
	Anticipated number of participants		Anticipated number of participants
	Individual and/or collective leadership within stakeholder groups		Individual and/or collective leadership within stakeholder groups
	Potential for economic gain or loss		Potential for economic gain or loss
	Potential for community impact/change		Potential for community impact/change
	Potential for social power gain or loss		Potential for social power gain or loss

Use the form on page 90 to help others help you. Make copies of this form and distribute them to your design team. Use the Formal/Informal table as the scale for rating the project. Have each member of your team score the project individually, then share the results. See if team members view the environmental conditions the same way. From this information determine the initial formality of your strategy and how your process design might be affected by this level of formality.

Selecting Tools and Techniques

Once the overall community involvement strategy is selected, agency staff must choose the tools and techniques that best fit the situation. Large group meetings, one-on-one talks, public hearings and community forums might all be applied as some time during a public involvement process. Combine and reconfigure the various tools to customize your design. Make it work for you and the communities engaged in the process.

Now, there are some choices to make.

You have a good sense of how formal or informal the process must be. You've developed your process goals and objectives and you know where you want to be when you're done. Your sponsor outlined the limits and boundaries that the group must honor, and you know the level of authority you have to manage the process. Finally, you've been provided tools, techniques and resources to do the job. It's time to complete the design.

Standing in the Future

Start from where you want to be in the future. Imagine the end of the public involvement process, and work backwards. That's right! Start from the end and work toward the beginning. You're objective is to gain "Approval by the Council of a library development policy," or "Public support for the design of a new pedestrian bridge to be built between two bickering neighborhoods currently separated by a freeway" or "Lights for the baseball diamonds at the local junior high school." All of these are the end results you and the community are trying to achieve.

So, what's the last thing that must occur before obtaining success? What's the next to the last thing? Continue until you reach the point where you are today. This is sometimes termed "back-door" planning or reverse engineering because you're working from where you want to be, and not from where you are.

State your goals and objectives. Visualize success. Now describe the activity that will occur just before you attain that success. After describing that activity, take another step backwards, toward where you are today. What was contained in that step? What work was involved that got you to that result? Take another step back. And another. And another until you're back to where you started. When you find yourself describing today's planning process, you've completed the first draft of the design.

Ask yourself, "Does the design make sense? Can it be accomplished? Is it realistic? What fatal errors are buried in the step-by-step process?"

Now, try the planning process again, but this time start from where you are, today, and work forward. As you work toward the end result described in your goals and objectives, make adjustments to the draft design. Did you add steps that you'd

"Most men occasionally stumble over the truth, but most of them pick themselves up and hurry off as if nothing happened."

—Winston Churchill

forgotten during the first round? If so, insert them. When you reach the final step that will give you the outcome you want, ask again, "Will this progression of steps and activities get the community where it needs to go? Can it be done with the time and resources we've been provided? Is it politically realistic? Will stakeholders see it as an honest and credible process?"

Continue to work backwards and forwards, iteratively, until the design answers the questions listed above in the affirmative.

To aid you in designing public involvement processes, use the tables describing various meeting and communication tools and techniques located in Appendix A and B as references, and the list of questions shown below to assess the viability of a public involvement design.

Assessing the Process Design

- Does the design make sense?

- Can it be done with the time and resources provided?

- Is the process realistic? Can it accomplish the desired objectives?

- Are there fatal errors buried in the process?

- Will it get the community where it needs to go?

- Is the design politically realistic?

- Will stakeholders see the design as honest and credible?

What Are the Messages?

Throughout the planning process all the stakeholder communities and parties involved with the process will be sending and receiving messages. Some of these messages will be in the form of written letters, memos and reports. Other messages will be sent verbally in meetings, over the telephone, through private conversations and even through the media. The quality and frequency of that communication is important and should support your messages. Below is a simple form that can be used to track the messages throughout the process. This form is for tracking messages, how often they are sent, and through what communication means.

Common Messages and Themes

Sending Messages

What do you think the stakeholders need to know?

Message   Frequency   Method of Communication

_____   _____   _____

_____   _____   _____

_____   _____   _____

_____   _____   _____

Receiving Messages

What do you think the stakeholders are hearing?

Message   Frequency   Method of Communication

_____   _____   _____

_____   _____   _____

_____   _____   _____

_____   _____   _____

Repeating Messages

The stakeholders have told us that...

Message   Frequency   Method of Communication

_____   _____   _____

_____   _____   _____

_____   _____   _____

_____   _____   _____

Verifying Messages

Our reliable sources hear that…

Message   Frequency   Method of Communication

_____   _____   _____

_____   _____   _____

_____   _____   _____

_____   _____   _____

Communication Tools

Chapter 6 contains a detailed discussion of communication vehicles that can be helpful in sending and receiving messages within the context of a public involvement process. There is also a table located in Appendix B that organizes the strengths and weaknesses of these various communication techniques.

Public Involvement Strategy and Process Design

The following is an example of a one-page community involvement strategy and design.

> *As a friend of mine once observed, "Most newspaper reporters will write a balanced story, but the headline editors aren't to be trusted."*

Improving Multifamily Apartments Taskforce

A group of neighborhood associations wants to improve the physical conditions of several large multifamily apartment complexes. To help these local volunteers in their efforts the City agrees to supply staff support, meeting facilities and materials to conduct a community-based planning process. The objective of this support is to help these citizen volunteers get organized and create an action plan.

An issue map will be completed. This includes up to 25 interviews with business interests, real estate owners and other community leaders to define the scope of the problem.

A series of three focus group sessions with area residents will be held to further define the problem and gather their feelings about what conditions need to be improved.

There will be continuous informal one-on-one discussions with community leaders that are geared toward uncovering additional facts regarding core problems and key factors leading to the neighborhood decline. It is hoped that these leaders will gather added support for a more inclusive discussion and a possible approach to change in the area.

A series of four structured, small-group discussions with representatives of all stakeholder communities will be held. The objective will be to determine the range of acceptable alternatives for improving conditions. Once alternatives are clear and have support from leaders, a single general meeting of neighborhood residents will be held to ask which options they would like to pursue.

From this large group meeting and from subsequent taskforce groups an action plan will be created. Community action teams will be assigned to implement a program of systemic change.

Things to Remember

- Develop an overall framework strategy that supports the goals and objectives of the process.

- Create project objectives that will guide the work elements in your plan.

- Develop project boundaries to keep the process within the limits of your authority and resources.

- Determine how much community involvement is really necessary. Don't overbuild the process.

- Create and test the messages the group wants to send.

Toxic Waste Dilemma

Disputes can't be resolved if key participants won't come to the table. For instance, in certain western states there are toxic waste dump sites left over from World War II and the Cold War era that continue to pollute the ground and air around chemical plants. These sites are either on company property or directly adjacent to that property, and it is documented that the plants once made these chemicals. For economic, political and legal reasons these companies will not admit they were ever involved such dumping. They will not admit being a potentially responsible party to the action.

Community groups and the federal government have been in court for years trying to force these companies to admit their role in dumping this waste and clean up the mess, but without success. The laws protecting the environment make it more advantageous for firms to pursue litigation rather than suffer the economic penalties of admitting fault. And while the wheels of justice continue to grind ever so slowly, the toxic materials polluting the ground and water continue to poison the people in the area.

Chapter 5:

Implementing the Process

The Story of Chicken Grove

At the meeting of the Citizens Review Committee, Harry and Sue showed them the research results. The numbers showed that the newly annexed part of Chicken Grove needed additional fire service capacity, and a new fire station at the recommended location could provide incident response times within the nationally accepted standards. The Committee really liked Sue's research methods. There were lots of charts with rows and columns of numbers showing population statistics, demographic data and incident history. They were really surprised at how the report provided data on response time scenarios under different conditions.

When Sue finished her report to the Committee, other Fire Department staff attending the meeting provided more detailed comment and support for Sue and Harry's recommendation. The Committee then asked the fire station location expert hired by Chicken Grove to review his assessment of Sue's findings. The consultant certified the results were accurate.

The Committee chair then stated that the "bottom line" was the recommended site met all the constraints and gave them a 15 percent cost advantage over all the other sites reviewed. With that the chairman asked if there was any other discussion on the matter, took a vote, and the Committee adopted the Fire Department's recommendation unanimously. A report stating the Committee's findings was forwarded to the Town Council along with the resolution to approve building the fire station.

What's Wrong?

As described above in the Chicken Grove Story, deployment of the community involvement process has become routine. If sponsors and agency staff have successfully completed projects using a particular public involvement model in the past, then they are likely to continue to use that model without regard to changes in the community, social or political environments. What Harry and Sue don't know is that there is a "sniper" waiting to ambush the process. Harry and Sue still believe they will successfully complete a fifth fire station without incident.

The following chapter examines options for implementing the community involvement process. It contains a toolbox full of ideas and job aids for practitioners. There is a step-by-step model included that incorporates concepts discussed in previous chapters. Suggestions and recommendations for surviving and thriving during community involvement implementation are incorporated as bullet points and checklists. After completing this chapter, the reader will have a practical understanding of action planning, project implementation, modifications of the plan during implementation, project assessment and long-term complicity building.

Questions to Frame Discussion

- What are the process objectives and how can they be achieved?

- What process expectations do the agency sponsor, the staff and the participants hold?

- What role can participants play in implementing and managing the public involvement process?

- Are there "snipers" waiting to ambush the process? If so, what is their agenda? Have they been invited to participate?

- What is an action plan and when should it be developed?

- How can project monitoring help you communicate?

- Why are milestones an important vehicle for measuring progress?

- What can you do to keep the communities and stakeholders involved?

Implementing the Process

Project deployment is the fourth stage of community involvement. It implements the Stage 3 design. Action planning is the primary tool used in the deployment process; project management skills are also required. During this stage resources are assigned, constraints are identified, and activities are put into clear, time-bound sequential order. Responsibility is also assigned so that specific tasks are linked to specific individuals. The action plan is put into motion.

As activities and tasks are completed, the project manager monitors and assesses progress, and modifies the action plan as necessary to keep on track. Difficulties will be encountered. Tools and techniques may need to change. Personnel assignments may change. Political, social and demographic conditions may change. The project manager must adapt the process and communicate changes to participants.

To help generate active support for the community involvement process, a small, representative group of participants from the process should be included in creating the action plan. As the need to change the action plan occurs, make sure those individuals are included in discussions.

Review the Objectives/Establish Clear Expectations

Review and clearly define the objectives of the community involvement process before starting the action plan. Make the objectives SMART. The more concrete and time-bound, the greater the likelihood of achieving the objectives.

Ask the project sponsor and participants for a clear definition of what they expect from the process and what standards of performance they want. Conflicts and

SMART

Specific
Measurable
Aggressive but Achievable
Results oriented
Time-bound

misunderstandings regarding the process' overall objective can create serious trouble. Consensus on direction may be difficult during the early stages of action planning, but don't proceed without a clear understanding of overall objectives and performance measures.

Action Planning

An action plan is a step-by-step recipe for accomplishing a specific objective. It is used to clearly identify what has to occur, it tests and validates the objective itself, and it is a way to communicate expectation to the people who are working the plan.

In addition, action planning establishes accountability for each task and reduces the chances of delays. Communicating the action plan also creates a discussion by the people involved in implementation and encourages their ownership of the process.

Always begin with the end in mind. As described in Chapter 4, work from where you want to be...to where you are, now.

Questions to Ask about Objectives and Expectations

- Why do we want to accomplish the objective?

- Does everyone agree on the objective? If not, can the objective be rewritten to gain agreement?

- Is there room for misunderstanding? Have we defined terms?

- Is the objective of manageable size and scope? If not, can we break the objective into smaller bites?

Questions:

- What is the need for and availability of resources? Is quality an issue?

- Are there any intangible resources needed that may not be immediately evident?

Defining Resources

Resources aren't just dollars and cents...they come in many forms, both tangible and intangible. People are resources and come as staff, volunteers, stakeholders and even "snipers." Tools and techniques are resources. Public trust and goodwill, community patience as discussions proceed, and political support to delay a decision...these are all resources. The time donated by process participants is a resource. The school cafeteria used to hold a public meeting is a resource. The food and beverages for that public meeting donated by the local supermarket are a resource.

Identifying Constraints

Let's be honest about the word "constraint." What's really being discussed are "problems." A guy named Murphy first identified the clinical features of problems. First, there will always be more problems than opportunities. Second, it's hard to identify all the problems before starting a project or process. Problems seem to lurk in the corners and they're hard to see. Third, if the process is delayed until all the problems are identified...the process will never get started. Assume that difficulties will pop up after that action plan is implemented.

Here is a practical way to identify as many as possible before starting:

Tangible constraints can be easily identified and quantified. They include things like lack of time, lack of money, lack of staff and lack of space, all of which are fairly evident to most project managers. Other tangible constraints may be outside the sight of the project planner, but are just as tangible, for instance, the unforeseen resignation of a key staff member. ***Intangible constraints*** might include poor participant attitudes, previous conflict between community members, and lack of political support. Many of these constraints will appear during the research stage of the process, yet because they are difficult to identify and even more difficult to quantify, intangible constraints may go undetected. Intangible constraints are difficult to overcome.

Manageable constraints are just that...they fall within the scope of the project's authority and influence, and can be resolved. ***Unmanageable constraints*** are recognized as being outside normal channels of authority and influence. They may or may not be resolvable, but they can often be either influenced or mitigated.

Classification of Constraints

	Tangible	Intangible
Manageable		
Unmanageable		

Questions to Ask About Constraints

- What are the constraints facing the public involvement process? What can be done to manage those constraints?
- Which constraints are controllable and which are not?
- What's the probability for overcoming a constraint?

Q: How do you eat an elephant?

A: One bite at a time.

Impatience with the Process

And speaking of difficulties, the process of public involvement is tedious. It takes time to do it right. On the agency side, most planners, engineers and administrators fail to include public involvement in their project schedules. If they do include an element for community discussions, it's usually too little and too late in the process to inspire stakeholders to thoughtful interaction. On the other hand, stakeholders may feel that the solutions are obvious "if these bureaucrats would only open their eyes and look." Community leaders may understand the need to go slow, but meeting participants just want to get in, make their pitch, and get out. People new to the public involvement process are skeptical that "it's all just window dressing and the decisions have already been made." Because of inexperience, participants leave the process (check out) before more productive discussions can begin. Seasoned community activists know this pattern and use it to their advantage. They wait for moderate community interests to get frustrated and leave the process, then they fill this vacuum in participation with their own agenda. In even more calculating scenarios, snipers seed discontent and encourage this exodus.

Avoid this systemic problem. Manage participant expectations. Prepare a complete schedule of activities and outcomes at the very beginning of the process. Distribute this schedule to all participants and explain that the process might be considerably slower and more tiresome than they would like. At the end of each event, remind participants of where they started, where they currently are in the process, what they've accomplished to date, what to expect at the next event, and an estimated time of achievement (ETA) for the process.

By classifying constraints they are at least acknowledged and with discussion by staff, clues to resolution may appear. "No one can guarantee the outcome of a public involvement process...but we should be able to assure there are no surprises!"

Project Milestones

A community involvement process can be a long, drawn-out affair. It helps maintain enthusiasm and trust in the process if milestones are established to gauge progress. Simply divide the project into discrete, logical pieces. During deployment one of the first milestones might be creating a critical stakeholders and communities list. Other milestones might be holding the first or last of several meetings, developing a list of critical issues for the group to consider, or completing the report recommending action to the City Council. It helps the project if milestones come at frequent intervals. Milestones also help chart and acknowledge progress, identify areas for additional work, and give early warning if delays are going to occur.

Questions to Ask About Milestones

- Are the milestones appropriately spaced along the time line?

- Do the milestones represent significant accomplishments?

- Can stakeholders and participants also participate in and celebrate milestones?

Tips for Tracking Progress

- Identify a milestone for each objective and each major activity.

- Create a written checklist of all the activities necessary for achieving these milestones.

- Include dates, deliverables and responsible parties on this checklist.

- Communicate performance expectations to people responsible.

- Update and distribute the chart frequently.

- Celebrate success: let people know they're making progress.

Creating Milestones

- Divide the project into discrete, logical pieces.

- Create outcomes and deliverables for each piece.

- Develop a calendar for achieving these outcomes.

- Highlight critical points where multiple deliverables must come together.

- Graphically indicate how the pieces might be dependent on each other.

Task Identification and Development

When assembling the tasks under an action plan, don't be too concerned with the order in which they go. Just try to think of all the activities needed to complete the milestone. Once you've identified all the tasks, go back and put them in the correct sequence.

Ultimately a project manager must decide what collection of activities and tasks, if completed, will lead to a successful project. Major milestones have already been established, so now each task leading to a milestone must be identified. This calls for a detailed, step-by-step accounting of all tasks. By each task there must be the name of the person responsible for completing the task. Likewise, there needs to be a specific date for completing that task.

Consider forming a public involvement team consisting of a representative from the agency sponsor, technical staff, and public involvement project staff. At some point you may even want to include key community leaders as team members.

Once a comprehensive list of actions is created on the action planning form, (see Appendix C, page 219) put each item in the order in which it must be completed. In the column marked "accountability" use people's names and not simply a position or title. Likewise, be specific as to the day, month and year the action is to be completed.

Remember: For each major action, a milestone is established. For each milestone a list of tasks or activities is developed. For each task, a person is held accountable for completing the activity and a time is set for completion.

Ways to make people feel included:

- Create a summary of "vital information" for stakeholders.

- Develop and maintain a list of names, addresses, e-mail and phone numbers of key participants.

- Display the project schedule at all events.

- Respond to questions and comments in writing…to everyone.

- Inform participants with timely meeting notes, group recommendations and project updates.

- Let people know when key issues are being considered.

- Ask for help from participants when additional work is required.

Tips for Action Planning

- Construct action plans in writing...in pencil; be suspicious of people creating first drafts in ink.

- Provide planning teams with initial starting points for action planning...do a draft to bring to the first meeting.

- List project assumptions to provide a foundation and context for understanding each step.

- Encourage people to challenge the assumptions.

- Describe expectations and outcomes clearly.

- Gain agreement from participants and stakeholders on the action plan before proceeding.

Underestimating the time needed to complete a task is a common mistake made by project staff. To create an initial cross-check, it is helpful to set an overall time frame for completing the project, and work "backwards" to set critical delivery dates. In the same way, use the times established to reach milestones to calculate timetables for tasks and activities.

By following the step-by-step model developed in this chapter, a project manager should have the first draft of an action plan ready to review. Ask, "Is this plan accurate, timely, and appropriate? Does it fit the needs of the project, process and stakeholders?" If everything appears to be in order after one iteration of the process...then something's wrong!

Go back and check all the tasks. What was left out? What isn't in the proper order? It's almost certain that something needs to change. So, make any appropriate changes to the first draft, and then take another crack at it. With each iteration the action plan will improve... become more realistic...more "do-able."

Things to Remember about Deploying the Process

Deployment:

- Don't get complacent about the need to involve people.

- Plan for snipers.

- Generate active support by using a small, representative group of process participants as part of the planning team.

Action planning:

- Action planning establishes accountability and reduces delays.

- Communicate the action plan to those responsible for implementation.

- Action plans must be in writing.

- Create a draft action plan as a starting point for group discussion.

- Gain some level of agreement from participants before initiating the action plan.

- Begin action planning using the end product as the focus.

- Clearly define your sponsor's objectives and the community's expectations of the process.

- Identify the resources required to undertake the project, including people and political support.

- Identify constraints and decide how to manage those constraints.

- Establish project milestones.

- Identify specific tasks.

- Estimate timeframes for performance.

- Review and modify the plan as needed.

- Monitor and track the progress of the action plan.

Chapter 6:

Meetings and Their Role in Community Involvement

The Story of Chicken Grove

As you now know, because of rapid general growth and the annexation of a large piece of county-owned land south of town, the Chicken Grove Fire Department needed to build a new fire station. The station would be located in the heart of the newly annexed area so that response times would be within acceptable limits.

The Town Administrator and Fire Chief initiated a request for the new fire station, but complicating this action was a recent state law that requires all cities and towns to post public notices in the newspapers and in the physical area of any significant capital improvements. In addition, the town had to hold a hearing before approving any public buildings and capital improvements.

Staff followed all the rules prescribed by the state for advertising the proposed project in the local paper and for constructing large zoning-type signs around the property letting the public know that change was coming. They brought the request for approval of the capital improvement project to the Town Council for their adoption. The Mayor and Town Council had been involved in the

process all along so when the time came for approval, no surprises popped up... except maybe one.

Just as the Mayor called the meeting to order and opened the topic of the fire station for discussion, a noise erupted from the hallway. The chamber doors flew open and in rushed fifty angry neighborhood activists carrying signs that said, "Recall the Mayor and Town Council", "Our children's safety comes first", "Beware of fire fighters bearing gifts" and "Keep dangerous, smelly fire trucks out of our neighborhood!"

The Mayor looked at the Town Administrator...the Town Administrator looked at the Fire Chief...and the Fire Chief looked at his staff.

"Holy cow! How did this happen?"

What's wrong?

What just happened in the Town Council Chambers is called a "blow out." The term aptly describes a confrontation between community interests where there are lots of shouting, raised voices, name calling, and even some profanity. Incivility is a nicer term for it, but "blow out" is probably more accurate. It's just short of physical violence.

In this case, the council meeting was the battleground for two civic interests: A group of organized protesters opposed to placing a new fire station in their neighborhood, and the professional managers who were proposing to change the neighborhood by adding a public amenity.

With conflict as described brewing, could this meeting have been managed in a civil and democratic manner? Some residents would say, "Protest and demonstration **are** part of the democratic process. When policy makers won't listen, protest is our only alternative!" Others would say that incivility and hostility are never acceptable ways to behave, and that law enforcement officers should have been called to quell the disturbance. In fact, the Town had options and didn't realize it.

Questions to Frame Discussion

Even though it cannot be assumed that a set of tools that worked well in one situation years ago will work well in today's highly charged and changing world, the following questions are provided to help focus this chapter's theme of bringing stakeholders into the decision-making process.

- Why was this citizen protest a surprise to the policy makers?

- Who organized this protest and why did they pick the council meeting for their demonstration?

- What could the town have done to minimize or eliminate the conflict, and redirect the protesters' energy into more productive activities?

- What actions can the Town take to recover from this controversy?

- How could the meeting have been designed to make a difference?

Meetings: A Primary Communication Vehicle

Much of the work described in this workbook centers on using meetings to communicate. This means that the people engaged in community involvement need a certain proficiency in planning and facilitating meetings. The following material should be used in conjunction with *Chapter 7, Managing Conflict and Mediating Community Disputes.*

The Importance of Meetings in Community Involvement

Meetings, whether held one-on-one, in small groups, or as large public events, are the dominant methods used to engage stakeholders in discussions about community issues. Meetings form a comfortable and reliable format in which people who may be at odds can come together and communicate their hopes, dreams and concerns. Everyday life is filled with meetings. They range from formal meetings with colleagues and peers to informal meetings with friends and family members.

That said, even though everyone knows how to hold meetings, being able to hold *good meetings* requires special skills. Ineffective meetings are usually due to poor planning or a lack of leadership. Most schools, colleges and universities do not teach people to plan and manage group meetings, so, like riding a bicycle, meeting management is a skill that is acquired through experience.

Two techniques that can be immediately applied to any meeting to get tremendous improvement is: 1) Always develop a detailed *agenda* in advance, and 2) always create an *action plan* at the end. The *agenda* is the road map or script that tells everyone what their role is and what is supposed to happen. Without the agenda the meeting has no direction, no beginning, no end and no purpose. A written *action plan* is vital to getting results from the meeting. Without an *action plan* that tells everyone who does what by when, the time spent in meetings is usually wasted.

Many meeting techniques are discussed in this chapter. Each has its own set of advantages and disadvantages, and each offers ways to engage groups and facilitate communication. Use these techniques creatively to develop new, novel ways of helping people find agreement.

It is critical for the people charged with engaging communities in problem-solving and planning to have the necessary skills to hold good meetings. Those skills include the ability to develop an agenda, to facilitate a group's discussions, and to complete an action plan at the end of a meeting. As this chapter proceeds, the reader is challenged to apply these three critical concepts to each type of meeting discussed.

Small, Medium and Large Group Meetings

It is important to distinguish between large, medium and small groups. Size is important to designing meetings and the techniques applied to groups, and size is relative to the purpose of the meeting. Very large groups of over 100 people require special tools. The techniques discussed in this book are most applicable to small and medium-sized groups.

A good meeting manager should be able to:

- Develop a detailed agenda in advance.

- Facilitate a group discussion.

- Create an action plan at the end.

The following definitions are provided to give the reader perspective on group size and application.

Small Group Meeting: Discussions with two to fifteen people fall into the category of small group meetings. These might include advisory committees or task forces appointed by an elected public body to investigate issues.

Medium Group Meeting: Depending on the type of meeting and objectives to be accomplished, a medium group might be from twelve to forty people. A public hearing with twenty-five people might be considered on the small side, but fifteen people in an intense workshop would be quite large.

Large Group Meeting: Anytime more than fifty people are in a meeting, it can be termed a large group meeting.

Anatomy of a Meeting

No matter the type, all meetings will have a beginning, middle, and end. On the surface this seems simplistic, but it is crucial that you understand the importance of these elements for a successful meeting. If participants feel 1) good about why they are attending the meeting, 2) that time will not be wasted, and 3) that their opinions will be respected, the meeting will be well received. This is why it is important to make participants feel comfortable right from the start.

Words have Power

Use appropriate words to either calm down or jazz up the group's energy. When people need an energy boost, try using active verbs in your facilitation. When people are overly excited, use passive verbs.

Beginning the Meeting

Start the meeting by introducing any new people and briefly discussing the ground rules. Clarify your policy on things like smoking, breaks, restrooms, telephones, beepers, and cell phones before the meeting starts. Define time expectations, and let the group help set time boundaries and limits for each discussion item. Encourage equal participation and clear, concise statements from participants.

Next, review the meeting agenda, what group performance is anticipated and what outcomes should come from the experience. Make sure the driving questions that frame the discussion are clear and familiar to the group.

During the Meeting

Here are some techniques that you can use to make your meetings run smoother.

- Use the driving questions to stimulate thought and discussion. Limit the number of driving questions discussed at one meeting, since subordinate questions will spontaneously occur and eat into the little time you have.

- Encourage alternative thinking. In addition, challenge the groups' creativity at the beginning of the meeting, and then bring them back to reality at the end. Support "out-of-the-box" thinking early on, but "right now, right here" when action planning and implementation are being discussed.

- Repeat participants' statements, key phrases and own words as the meeting proceeds. Keep the group focused and the meeting on track by repeating earlier group directions and decisions. "Earlier I heard you and the group reach this decision, so how does this conversation support that decision?"

- Facilitators may find it difficult to record the substantive portion of a meeting and also attend to the interpersonal and process needs of the group, so consider having someone act as a record keeper.

- Use mildly conciliatory phrases to help organize and clarify issues. For instance: "While sympathetic to the concerns of the black hats, the group supports the view of the white hats."

- Frequently ask participants to summarize meeting points as the session progresses.

- Positive affirmations can precede normative recommendations. For instance, "It seems like you're making progress. What <u>should</u> the group do in this instance?"

- When consensus is gained, the facilitator should restate that understanding and determine if the group still agrees.

- Take bio-breaks. Most people can last 1½ to 2 hours before requiring a break.

- Breaks provide opportunities for off-line conversations. It's amazing how much can be resolved on a 15-minute break.

- Facilitators have a contract with the people in a group. If the group starts on time, they need to finish on time.

- A good facilitator **does not** allow personal opinions to enter into the discussion.

- Groups can sense stress, fatigue and fear in a leader. The facilitator should work hard to avoid those feelings, and should strive to keep energized. Have fun and enjoy the meeting process.

After the Meeting

Once the formal meeting is over, the facilitator's job is not done. He or she needs to tie up loose ends or the great results obtained from the participants could dissolve. After the meeting, the facilitator will want to debrief with the meeting sponsor or leader to evaluate results, determine if any subtle points were missed, and identify the next steps in the process. Document the meeting in a written report.

Collecting Data

It is paramount that you collect data and document the process, both during and after a meeting. The facilitator receives volumes of information from the participants, so it is important to capture and organize what the participants say. If not, they will question whether or not you really care about their ideas. It is common for a facilitator to use flip charts during the meeting, but a person taking notes is a better choice. Story boards and data cards are a favorite because the technique calls on participants to write their own meeting notes.

Unless required by the jurisdiction, it is recommended that audio recording of community involvement meetings not be part of normal practice. Once an audio tape is created, it becomes a public record and must comply with regulations for preservation. Tape recordings rarely help clarify misunderstandings and they may raise more questions than they answer. Summary notes of discussions, points of agreement and disagreement, and decisions are preferred. They cost less and are easily communicated.

Planning for Action

Action planning occurs as part of daily life. Examples of informal action plans might include a grocery list, a food recipe and a list of shopping errands. An action plan is simply a step-by-step inventory for accomplishing specific objectives. It is important to understand how using action plans to identify critical activities and listing tasks to complete can support the overall project. Formal, written action planning is time consuming and normally reserved for special projects.

Action planning clearly identifies what has to occur if you are to accomplish your objective. It tests and validates the objective itself by answering the question, "Is the objective truly achievable? Finally, action planning breaks the objective into smaller pieces, and checks and tests reality.

With action planning you communicate what is expected to those who need to know. By determining accountability for each of the action steps, you reduce the chances of delays or voids in the pursuit of the objective. In addition, by effectively communicating the action plan you create dialogue among the participants and encourage ownership of the project.

Any time a group or multiple groups of people must work together, writing a formal action plan should be considered. This is especially true when the group's goals and objectives require multiple tasks over a long period of time, and when the consequences of failure or the benefits of success are overwhelming.

Writing Great Questions

Use driving questions to focus a group's attention and energy when working on complex topics. These driving questions are developed in advance of meetings and mandatory when facilitating decision-making meetings, focus group research sessions, and organizational dispute intervention. Carefully planned and crafted driving questions can be the difference between meeting failure and success, between the group achieving consensus and clear direction, or continued divisiveness and conflict. Poorly developed driving questions will lead groups to circular thinking and frustration.

You should keep a few simple rules in mind as you create driving questions. First, driving questions should be broad enough to cover the full range of topics, but detailed enough to focus the group's attention. There are more detailed, subordinate questions embedded within the driving question. These subordinate questions are also written with care.

Next, a good driving question should frame the outcomes and decisions that need to be made at the end of the discussion. It should give participants clear, unambiguous boundaries regarding what is within discussion limits and what is not.

Finally, driving questions should not lead or steer the group toward a predetermined answer, and taken together, all the driving and subordinate questions should weave a theme through the fabric of the meeting.

Examples of Driving Questions:

Driving Question:

- What action should the County Parks Department take to include school children in discussions of new park facilities design?

Subordinate Questions:

- Who are the school children that would want to participate in design discussions?

- Are there legal or practical limitations to school children participating in design discussions?

- Where would the Department locate prospective participants?

- How can we encourage student participation?

- How will we modify our current community participation processes to allow student participation?

- Could students receive class credit for participation?

What constitutes a good driving question?

In developing good driving and subordinate questions, first assess the level of understanding of participants about the specific topic. The driving question can be more specific and detailed if the overall understanding of the participants about the subject matter is higher. Driving questions can survey for facts and concrete analysis of those facts. If, however, the group has little or no understanding of the topic, then the driving questions need to be global and built around perceptions, beliefs and feelings.

Keep the questions straight-forward and simple. Make each question compact. Use as few words as possible. Focus the question on one topic, thought or issue. Avoid questions that the group can answer with a simple "yes" or "no". Open-ended questions stated in neutral terms are best. Do not create questions where the answer is obvious. Likewise, there would be very few instances where rhetorical questions would be appropriate.

When working with new groups or conducting focus group research, rehearse the different ways to ask the questions. Make sure the questions will be understandable to participants. Listen to how the questions sound. Will vocal inflections influence a predetermined answer? Will cadence or pacing affect the group's response?

Put the questions in writing and allow participants to not only hear but see the words as they are read. If possible, place the driving questions on flip-charts, overhead slides or storyboards so they can be displayed at appropriate times during the discussion. This will visually help participants focus their comments.

If working in multiple sessions, with more than one facilitator or conducting ongoing focus group research, make sure all groups are addressing the same questions worded in the same way. Because words have such tremendous power, even the slightest change in wording can make a big difference in the meaning of the question to the listener.

During the meeting, use the driving questions like anchors to keep the group's attention focused on the topic. Repeat it frequently. When the discussion goes too far astray, ask the group, "How does your conversation help us answer the driving question?"

A Step-by-Step Model for Creating Driving Questions

The following is a practical, step-by-step method to help you develop driving questions. This process assumes you are working alone on these questions. The process described below can be applied with minor modification when working in group settings.

1. On one sheet of paper, white-board or flip-chart, list the overall information that the group needs to generate during the meeting.

2. On a separate sheet of paper, white-board or flip-chart, quickly brainstorm some specific questions to be answered by the end of the meeting. Leave lots of space between questions for reworking them later.

3. Ask yourself, "Are there similarities between the questions? What links can be found between the two lists? What themes are emerging?"

Body Language

When listening to a participant, make good eye contact but be careful how you nod your head. If you nod slowly it says, "I'm hearing what you're saying and we have connected." If you nod too rapidly participants may think you're saying, "I agree with you."

4. Give each of the themes an identified descriptive name and write a broad driving question that reflects the theme. Develop subordinate questions that fall logically from each of the driving questions. Continue this process until a level of detail appropriate to the meeting goals has been reached.

5. Find someone familiar with the topic to act as a "guinea pig." Try each of the questions on the test participant to determine if they are clear, simple, direct and focused. Rewrite any questions that fail the test.

6. Look at all the questions you've developed. Place them in a logical sequence so that the answer to one will give participants a basis for answering the next. If there are any concerns about running out of time, prioritize the driving questions.

7. During the session, be prepared to eliminate subordinate questions that are nice to have answered but not necessary to the final product.

With the number of business meetings and research sessions held daily, the costs of just one meeting can mount up to thousands of dollars in salaries and forgone opportunities. For this reason, it is important to make the most of the limited time groups have to decide important issues by creating clear, focused driving questions. Developing high quality driving questions is more time consuming than difficult, and the process requires a lot of planning.

Open Meetings

Open meeting laws protect the public from community decisions being made without citizen oversight. In the past, decisions on public issues were made behind closed doors, conflicts of interest were not disclosed, and confidence in public officials was eroded. In the early 1970s, most states passed legislation requiring all meetings of public bodies to be posted in advance of the meeting giving anyone who wanted to watch the opportunity to do so. Many local governments have policies that citizens not only have the right to watch but can make substantive comments about proceedings.

State and federal laws have become more prescriptive of the ways jurisdictions administer open meetings. To avoid violations, the agency must pay close attention to the process. Open meetings laws are not difficult to manage, but even minor errors can embarrass public officials, invalidate the decisions made, and create distrust between the agency and the community. Each state's laws differ slightly regarding what constitutes an open meeting and how those meetings must be advertised, noticed, documented, and managed. It is important to check your local requirements.

Any meeting in which an elected or appointed public body could have a substantive discussion, or make a decision may constitute a public meeting. If public business could take place, open meeting laws take effect and the meeting is open for the public to watch. Anytime a public body could assemble with a quorum present, there is a good chance the open meeting laws apply. In some states, no

Reminders for satisfying open meeting requirements:

- Public bodies are bound by open meeting laws and are required to give advance notice and posting of public meetings.

- Postings must state the group, the date, the time and the location of the meeting.

- An agenda must be developed in advance that states what is pending for discussion and decision.

- No decision can be made outside of an open meeting.

- If an item isn't listed on the agenda, it should not be discussed.

- Go beyond the letter of the open meeting law in community involvement processes.

two elected policy makers can discuss an issue that could come to their attention or vote without posting an open meeting notice.

Unfortunately, because of the highly structured nature of open meeting laws, it may be difficult to find consensus positions within that format. By necessity there may be limited opportunities for public participation, discussion and debate, and much like typical public hearings, speakers may try to polarize the discussion and "play the crowd" when presenting their positions.

In satisfying open meeting requirements, keep the following few things in mind. Although not all government meetings are open to the public, all elected public bodies are bound by open meeting laws. These laws require advance notice and posting of, and public access to, most meetings where a policy board could make decisions affecting the public. The postings must state, at minimum, the group, the date, the time, the location of the meeting, and frequently any matters pending that are scheduled to be heard and could be decided by the group.

An agenda must be developed in advance of the meeting. It usually states the issues to be discussed, in what order that discussion will occur, and what, if any, decisions might be made. When open meeting laws apply, no decisions can be made outside the formal structure, so if an item or issue that isn't listed on the agenda is raised, don't discuss it. You might even go beyond the letter of the open meeting law in community involvement processes by accommodating public participation in the meeting. Always make meeting times and locations as convenient to the public as possible and be sensitive to the public's right to attend.

The Florida HOA

Two women were sitting poolside in the sun at their condominium. One woman said to the other, "What do you think of the new maintenance company? I'm really not satisfied with the way they're cutting the hedges at the entrance." The other woman turned to her friend and said, "Yes, I think we should do something about that." Unfortunately, one of their neighbors had been eavesdropping. Later that day they received a call from the district attorney asking both women to meet him in his office the next morning.

When they arrived, he asked them about their pool conversation. After they admitted having the talk, he explained that they had violated the state's open meeting law. Since both women were elected members of the Homeowner's Association Board, since they had had a conversation about an issue that might be discussed and decided at a future meeting, and since they had not seen fit to post their conversation as an open meeting 24 hours in advance with an agenda, they had violated a Florida state law.

Lesson: As an elected official, know your state's unique open meeting law conditions.

Reminders for satisfying open meeting requirements:

- Meeting times and locations need to be as convenient to the public as possible in order to be sensitive to the public's right to attend.

- Minutes and notes from public meetings should be processed and available in a timely manner.

Some Effective Meeting Types and Techniques

Meetings are costly and time consuming, so selecting the right meeting type for the right situation is important. Some meetings are better for collecting information, while others do well at stimulating creative thinking, and still other meetings promote debate and decision making. Because communities are different, a meeting that worked very well in one place may not be effective in another. The following material outlines several types of meetings and describes their strengths and weaknesses in accomplishing different objectives.

One-on-One Meeting

Individual meetings with community leaders and opinion-makers can be a very effective way of communicating. These meetings should take place early in the planning process as part of the research and data-gathering effort. They can be used to determine concerns and problems early enough so you can factor them into a resolution. When using one-on-one meetings, it is important to include not only those who will be affected by a decision, but also those who perceive themselves as being affected by the decision or problem. Invite everyone to contribute views, give advice, and make comments.

One-on-one meetings are not necessarily "secret" events so you should document them by keeping a log of who attended and what they said. Unfortunately, one-on-one meetings can lead to a charge of ex parte communication. Keep good records just in case an issue arises.

The advantages of one-on-one meetings include getting to know stakeholders and the communities they represent, creating a public record of agency efforts, identifying problems that may not be fully evident, and opening personal two-way communication, which can lead to future consensus. The cost of one-on-one meetings is the on-going staff time they require to develop and nurture the relationships.

Workshops

Workshops are time-limited events held to discuss some specific topic and achieve a particular purpose. Workshops often involve interactive, hands-on activities that are designed to maximize the chances of achieving defined outcomes. They may be limited to small groups of pre-selected and screened participants, or could be structured to include hundreds of participants that focus on a limited number of specific questions. Workshops are not subject to strict parliamentary procedures and try to encourage creative, solutions-based communication. In workshop settings, participants must have the opportunity for a free and open discussion. Workshops can be done in various formats and venues and may be completed in just one meeting or can be extended to multiple sessions.

Workshops can be very effective in identifying problems, clarifying key issues, and finding consensus. Unfortunately, workshops require high levels of staff support to accommodate a relatively limited number of people. The detailed written materials and staff time required to hold a quality workshop mean high costs.

Community Forums

Community forums encourage participants to give voice to specific ideas and concerns about topics where direction is undefined, or where the issues having an impact on a decision are ambiguous. These meetings are widely advertised to gain the greatest number of participants. Each person wishing to contribute to the discussion has the opportunity to make a presentation to the group. A third-party facilitator runs the meeting to assure balance, and in some cases, TV and media coverage is encouraged to assure broader input from the community.

Public forums give each group of stakeholders the opportunity to hear the views of the other affected interests. This type of meeting also allows the ultimate decision makers to get to know the stakeholders and the range of issues they represent. In doing so, staff and policy makers have the advantage of uncovering previously unidentified issues and problems.

Public forums are relatively expensive to hold and advertise, in terms of both money and staff time. Because emotions run high, the media often attends public forums hoping to catch a story. Participants can use public forums to gain media attention and solicit constituents. Provocative statements and highly charged language is par for the course. Controlling snipers and opportunists during a public forum takes a skilled facilitator.

Public Hearings

Public hearings are formal meetings convened by either elected or appointed officials. Public hearings have legal requirements for timing, location, and the processes attached to them. Changes in zoning and land use, imposition of taxes, adoption of budgets, and public policies that have broad, important consequences may require a public hearing.

The methods used to conduct public hearings may be prescribed by statute or may simply be a product of custom and local preference. Traditional public hearings are probably the least effective way officials can discuss issues, offer alternatives, and gain consensus on matters of public and community interest.

Public hearings generally consist of a summary of main points by agency staff, an outline of the range of possible decisions or solutions, and a period of time for those attending the hearing to comment on proposed solutions. During the comment period, people are called one at a time to a microphone facing the dais, and they are given a limited amount of time to make their points. One after another, speakers either repeat or dispute what the previous speaker said. In the end, people have talked *at* one another—not *with* one another, and little real progress toward an agreeable resolution has been made.

The fact is, public hearings are usually legal requirements for spending public resources. Given the highly structured, ritualistic nature of a typical public hearing, they offer few opportunities for productive public dialogue. To get an issue to the point where a public hearing is required, there must already be a strong recommendation on the matter. Polarity is established. Confrontation, conflict, and long-term community divisiveness may be the result. The potential to generate any type of productive consensus is limited. The typical public hearing where strong feelings exist wastes time and divides the community. Unfortunately, it's required!

On the positive side of public hearings, some jurisdictions have taken steps to add alternative methods for taking comment and reducing acrimony. For instance, in some places a court reporter may be employed to take one-on-one comment from the public. This technique reduces the number of impassioned orators whose sole purpose is to whip the gathered crowd present in the council chambers (or on cable TV) into a frenzy.

Body Language

If a participant is being disruptive or dominating the conversation, when do you know you have the group's permission to cut them off? Wait until you see other participant's eyes roll. Then you know you have permission to act. Watch the eyes.

Tips for CAPs

- Establish clear performance boundaries and create a CAP mission.

- Give the group time frames for completing their work.

- Hold regular periodic meetings to assure the CAP stays current on issues.

- Provide high-quality staff support.

- Appoint a seasoned leader.

- Train the CAP members in basic planning and meeting techniques.

- Monitor frequently for "mission creep."

Community Advisory Panels (CAP)

Another way to include the community in decision making is to form an advisory panel or committee. The community advisory panel (CAP) takes on the tasks of developing and evaluating alternative proposals as well as reviewing technical data. Their work generally results in recommendations that are forwarded to staff and/or the policy board.

Although most CAPs are formed as a result of legislative or regulatory mandates, legal obligation is not the only reason to construct them. There are many practical reasons for, and benefits from, using CAPs including: 1) blue-ribbon support for the policy board to take action on a project, 2) the wisdom that groups can bring to a decision, and 3) the endorsement of a decision by community members.

The leadership of, and staff support for, the CAP should provide members with a mission, a clear understanding of their role and project boundaries, and the type of information they are expected to provide. Before establishing a CAP, it may be beneficial to review the status of other current committees and determine what's worked and hasn't worked in the past. Try to limit the CAP to 25 members or fewer. The membership should reflect the community it represents. This can be achieved by having members appointed by the governing body with recommendations from stakeholders and staff.

Open Houses

An open-house event provides participants with information through an open, flowing and loosely structured one-on-one discussion process. Concerned and interested community members can meet informally with a myriad of staff, experts, policy makers, and citizens in a warm and encouraging atmosphere. The process can be the starting point for healing severely divided communities. This meeting technique can also be very helpful in building a sense of community where none currently exists.

The objective is to give information, facts and figures, and take from participants their beliefs, feelings, perceptions, dreams, fears and suggestions. The open-house process is highly interactive with technical people and policy makers fielding questions from community stakeholders on the spot, one-on-one or in small groups. In addition, a portion of the meeting can be devoted to more formal, large group presentations.

Graphic representations, charts, pictures and hand-outs are supplied to encourage communication. Information flows both to and from the participants, and content experts, policy makers and peers are all subject to questioning. At the meeting, people familiar with all facets and features of the problem or issue have a booth or table to visually display detailed information.

Part of the open house may also be dedicated to taking written or verbal comments and suggestions on the various alternatives to a project, plan or decision. There are many ways to capture participant comments for later use. Detailed feedback can be as formal as verbatim notes taken by court reporters, or as informal as

> *"I either want less corruption, or more chance to participate in it."*
>
> —Ashleigh Brilliant

personal, hand-written messages on Post-It-Notes placed on pictures or flip charts. When capturing participant comments during an open house, you are limited only by time and creativity.

Hold open-house events in an informal, familiar but appropriate setting at a time that is convenient to all. This means occasionally holding multiple open-house events on the same topic at different times and locations. Events should be advertised widely through the media, but it helps to notify people through informal channels, as well. Broad involvement is encouraged, but specific populations may also be targeted for attendance.

On the positive side of this technique, an open-house event encourages one-on-one discussions. Concerned and interested community members can meet with a raft of informal staff, experts, policy makers and citizens in a warm and encouraging atmosphere. The process can be the starting point for healing severely divided communities. This meeting technique can also be very helpful in building a sense of community where none currently exists. The open house is a flexible format that allows policy makers and stakeholders to get to know and understand each other and identify problems. The process nurtures credibility for both the agency and the community involvement process. It also limits the opportunity for mass confrontation.

On the negative side, open-house events may be expensive to produce in terms of both materials and time. To be convenient, the agency might have to sponsor multiple open houses at different locations and at different times. Community advocates often resent the open-house format because it normally does not allow for mass demonstrations. They find it more difficult to assemble blocks of supporters during the meeting to lobby for or against a specific direction.

Use the open-house meeting during the early stages of project development and community involvement. Make it part of the convening and scoping process.

Town Meetings

Town meetings are a mix of several techniques, including workshops, community forums and public hearings. In colonial times, the town meeting was the way public decisions were made, and with representative democracy, the town meeting evolved to a structured method for policy makers to stay in touch with constituents. Town meetings can be used to gain information and direction on broad public issues. This meeting technique must be well advertised to get the broadest participation and should be conducted in a semi-formal setting so that participants have a chance to see their public officials and ask them questions, but a sense of civility is maintained.

Town meetings are good for hearing views of stakeholders and for helping staff and policy makers see issues through the eyes of a constituent. If conducted at the early stages of a public project, alterations in direction can result. The downside to town meetings is a modest cost in terms of time. Much like public hearings, the town meeting may be perceived as promoting a pending decision and can damage the agency's credibility if handled incorrectly. When conducting town meetings, the opportunity for "stump" speeches and individual posturing should be limited. As with other types of formal discussions, incivility can be a problem. Officials are cautioned to refrain from answering questions on the spot. The recommendation is to have policy makers listen more than they talk during town meetings.

Charrettes

Charrettes are specialty meetings traditionally used by architects and planners to display design or planning concepts for constructing buildings or implementing plans. The concept of charrettes can be applied to other types of community involvement, planning and problem-solving if the ideas, problems or issues can be displayed visually. If it can be represented visually, then the charrette model can be used to gather information from the public. Examples include urban design, streetscapes, neighborhood redevelopment, traffic flow and circulation or interior space.

In a charrette, pictures, drawings, computer graphics and photographs are displayed to demonstrate a concept. These materials show how an area or building might look or work. Participants then comment on what they see. A feature of the charrette that makes it a good tool for community involvement is "real time" data collection. Participants can look at a plan, map or drawing, pick up a marker and put their thoughts and feeling on the document. Charrettes can quickly and easily gather community input.

Code Phrases: Important Tools for Facilitators

The following are some code phrases that you can use to keep community groups focused and on schedule during meetings. These terms and phrases help facilitators hold more productive meetings, but you need to use them with caution. The facilitator's primary directive is to preserve everyone's self-esteem. Some of the meanings listed under the code phrases are very blunt.

To Generate Clarity and Avoid Digression and Rambling

Code Phrase: "Could you simplify your comment so that I can understand it better?"

Meaning: • You are getting too technical.

• Your argument is too complex.

• You need to break the idea into smaller pieces so we can understand it.

Code Phrase: "That's very interesting, but could you help me connect your comment to the question we're currently trying to answer?"

Meaning: • You are digressing or rambling.

• Please relate your comment to the topic being discussed at this time.

Code Phrase:	"Would you help me summarize what you mean by that last comment?"
Meaning:	• You are rambling. Please make your point so we can move on to the next speaker.
	• Does your train of thought have a caboose?
Code Phrase:	"Can you list the key points of your comment so we can all understand them?"
Meaning:	• Your arguments are confusing. Try to summarize them so we can understand how they relate to the topic.

To Control Time and Keep Individuals from Monopolizing the Meeting

Code Phrase:	"In the interest of time..."
Meaning:	• You are violating the agreed time limits.
	• We are falling behind schedule and need to move on.
	• Please try to be brief and summarize your questions and comments.
Code Phrase:	"We need to hear from some folks who have not expressed an opinion yet."
Meaning:	• You are monopolizing the discussion. Please allow others to voice their thoughts, too.

To Handle Anger or Aggression within a Meeting

Code Phrase: "You seem to feel very strongly about that issue. Can you tell the group why?"

Meaning:
- You seem agitated. It may be helpful to verbalize the anger, and by doing so, resolve it.
- Help us understand why the issue makes you so angry.

Code Phrase: "You seem angry about the issue. Pretend I'm the person who made you angry and that it's safe to give me a piece of your mind. What would you say?"

Meaning:
- Man, you're really torqued! Right now it's probably better that you yell at me than yell at them. Let me have it!

Code Phrase: "Please direct your comments through me from now on."

Meaning:
- Listen, it doesn't help to get into a shouting match with another participant. I have promised to protect everyone at this table from threats and verbal assault.
- What you are doing is potentially destructive to the group process, so in the interest of your personal safety, yell at me!

Code Phrase: "Ohhhh, will someone pull that arrow from my heart?" (use appropriate gesture here)

Meaning:
- You took a "cheap shot." Sarcasm isn't a productive way to communicate your feelings.

Body Language

Use Silly Putty to help participants focus on controversial topics. Most people find it difficult to deal with conflict unemotionally. The excess emotion can build up and come out in inappropriate ways. A small egg of Silly Putty provided to each participant can help release energy. Don't even tell people why they have the Putty…they will intuitively know to open the egg and start squeezing the goo.

- If you must send "zingers," direct them toward me so the other participants won't feel the need to respond to your childish, unproductive comment.

To Reduce the Occurrence of Side Conversations

Code Phrase: "I'm having trouble hearing (understanding) the conversation."

Meaning:

- You are being rude to the speakers. There are side conversations taking place that confuse the listeners. We need to show respect for and listen to each speaker. Please avoid side conversations.

Code Phrase: "Can someone help me understand what was just said?"

Meaning:

- You are interrupting one another. We agreed that only one person will speak at a time.

To Remind Participants of Their Meeting Contract

Code Phrase: "Do we need to renegotiate our contract concerning how we operate this meeting?"

Meaning:

- The group is consistently violating a meeting contract provision and we need to either keep the contract or decide to modify it.

Code Phrase: "It appears that I'm not doing my job very well. Do we need to renegotiate our meeting contract?"

Meaning:

- The facilitator is allowing violations of the meeting contract by participants. We need to either keep the contract or agree to the modifications so there is a level playing field.

Other Methods for Communicating with and Engaging Stakeholders and Communities

Only imagination and budget stand in the way of finding great ways to communicate with stakeholders and participants in a community involvement process. The following are some examples of techniques that reside outside traditional meeting formats.

Newsletters

For long-term projects, newsletters can be a very effective tool for maintaining broad community involvement. They give a sense of stability and legitimacy to the agency and the community involvement process, and stakeholders receive periodic communication on which they depend.

To be effective, newsletters must be sent to participants on a regular basis. Their short, newspaper-like articles keep participants and stakeholders informed of project developments. They are good ways to announce meeting times, dates, and proposed agendas. You can also use them to summarize group progress and release new information about issues or problems facing a community.

Unfortunately, newsletters are relatively expensive to produce and can be criticized as being nothing more than agency propaganda and a waste of public money. Maintaining a list of current participants can be difficult and time consuming.

Tips for Using Newsletters

- Newsletters should contain facts and news of material interest to the reader. Keep the communications honest. Don't simply repeat the "party line" in hopes that people will start to believe it.

- Good news is easy to discuss in a newsletter, but bad news, project delays, mistakes and embarrassments are more difficult. Don't avoid the bad news, but rather use the newsletter to manage how difficulties are perceived.

- Avoid technical terms and jargon whenever possible.

- Pictures, diagrams, charts and graphs enhance communication.

- A special introductory issue should be created to give people as they join an ongoing project or process. Make extra copies. Give the introductory issue to policy makers and the press when they need to be given an overall orientation to the project.

Tips for Using Newsletters

- Periodically update the mailing list. Add new names and purge names of people no longer wanting the newsletter. Check on the names and addresses of mail returned to you.

- If significant numbers of participants do not speak English, be prepared to translate the newsletter into their primary language.

- Use newsletters to encourage community members to make their views and needs known. Include comment and survey forms to solicit feedback.

- Electronic newsletters and surveys are becoming more and more popular as greater numbers of people use the Internet.

There are a variety of ways to distribute newsletters, depending on the type of newsletter you've created and the stakeholders/participants you need to reach. Traditionally newsletters are mailed, but as postal rates increase, more and more agencies are using alternative distribution methods. Door hangers delivered by volunteers with nonprofit organizations are now popular. You can have small newsletters inserted into utility bills. You can send internal newsletters as payroll inserts, or place special section inserts in local newspapers. The Internet is fast becoming a low-cost alternative way to distribute newsletters.

In some communities you need a permit to deliver door-hangers or hand bills. Make sure that whatever material is delivered remains on the door knob or in the hands of the residents. When the information you so carefully assembled becomes street trash after a strong wind blows it away from its intended target, the town administrator will be calling your office with citizen complaints.

Speakers Bureaus

Speakers bureaus are small groups of well-informed, poised and confident staff or volunteers who prepare short, well-considered presentations about a specific topic. They provide diverse groups of listeners with a clear, unified, consistent message about the project, issue or problem at a relatively low cost. You can use speakers bureaus to maintain agency legitimacy and also correct errors in public perception.

Clubs, civic and social organizations, homeowners associations, schools, churches, chambers of commerce, PTA's, professional and trade organizations, neighborhood groups and employers all need speakers to inform and entertain the members at monthly luncheons, dinners and meetings. Because of the civic nature of community involvement processes, the topics an agency wants to discuss are ones that the community groups want and need to understand. There is a natural affinity between civic organizations and community involvement.

With speaking opportunities, you open an important path for two-way communication. At these engagements your speakers create an important channel for getting as well as giving information. Make sure your speakers are prepared with driving questions that will evoke thoughts and ideas. An additional benefit is that you will establish on-going, face-to-face relationships with the leaders of these neighborhood groups and civic organizations.

Tips for Developing Speakers Bureaus:

- Create clear messages and uniform ways of presenting them.

- Rehearse and polish the presentation with the group; look for ways to improve.

- Spice up the message with visual aids (overhead slides, PowerPoint presentations, 35mm slide photos, photographs, three-dimensional materials, videotapes or computer animation.

- If the topic is a physical project, arrange for a group site tour.

- Speakers bureaus require significant time commitments from both staff and volunteers. Make sure there are enough individuals to support the demand. Don't let people get burned out through overuse.

- Use these speaking opportunities to give and get information; work off-line with group leaders to get official endorsements or active support.

- Conclude the presentation with questions to the group. Obtain information from them as well as giving them the information you want them to receive.

Tips for Managing Hotlines:

- Document the question or comment and either answer the question, or explain to the caller what you are going to do, and when you will get back with him/her.

- Keep a detailed log.

- Inform caller of other communication avenues.

- Always give accurate information. If the answer is "I don't know," then make sure the question is referred to someone who can give a definitive answer.

- To be effective, the phone number must be widely advertised.

Neighborhood Tea and Coffee

Neighborhood teas and coffee klatches sponsored by community involvement participants establish the fact that project staff are willing to go into, and be a part of the community. Community members feel a greater sense of comfort and more relaxed. This improves communication. They will be more candid and personal in their discussions.

Generally, a formal presentation is unnecessary. During teas and coffees it is more important for project staff to listen to what is being said than to enter into a discussion or debate. Listen more and talk less.

Hotline Phone Number

Use hotline and information phone numbers to gather targeted information and control rumors. The caller reports a problem, situation, or rumor. The person answering takes the caller's name and number, and assigns the question to someone for a substantive response. Timely follow-through is critical to successful hotlines.

This technique can be a quick and easy way to establish communication with the broader community. It also fills the gap when a community member just needs to talk to a real person.

The downside to hotlines is that they can be expensive to maintain with a live person to answer the telephone. Costs can be reduced if an answering machine is used in place of an answering service. Automated information lines are less costly but people are less likely to utilize them. If you choose to use an automated service, manage caller expectations by calling it an "information line".

Hotlines and information lines are fast being replaced by the Internet with the easy access to web sites and e-mail.

Project Web Sites and Online Comment Forms

The Internet is a new and emerging avenue for reaching people. A web site outlining information about the project can give community members easy access to important information. In addition, this format can reach those persons who would otherwise remain silent, leaving valuable resources undiscovered. Online comment forms give people the ability to voice opinions and concerns, as well as volunteering material on additional resources.

Ombudsman

An ombudsman is staff member assigned to respond to questions and complaints from the public in a timely manner, and to help people move through the bureaucracy to resolve their complaints. Often the ombudsman will be the person on the receiving end of a telephone hotline. If so, apply the techniques outlined under "hotline."

The difference between a hotline telephone operator and an ombudsman is that the ombudsman has authority to work with others to resolve community problems during a project. The ombudsman can cut through red tape, make binding commitments and apply limited resources to getting things fixed. Problems occur when the ombudsman cannot meet community expectations, or commits to a resolution that is unacceptable to the sponsor.

The ombudsman walks a tight rope between the community and the jurisdiction. They are in a difficult position and are cautioned to "under commit and over perform."

Neighborhood Block Parties/Community Fairs

Close off a section of street, bring out the food, barbecue grills, lawn chairs, and turn up the music. It's party time! Block parties can quickly energize communities to initiate a community involvement process. They can also be the "celebration of success" event at the end of the process. This technique takes careful planning and a willing host or hostess but can be a terrific energizer for a community involved in civic discourse, a neighborhood project, or some other type of community process. The less structured and more spontaneous, the better.

An extension of the block party is the community fair. Often civic organizations will sponsor such fairs to gather people from all over a jurisdiction that share a common interest. It may be a recreational affiliation or some common civic improvement. Staff should monitor, participate in and sponsor community fairs whenever possible. It's a chance to promote the messages you want the community to hear, and to hear from the communities that you support.

Block parties and community fairs, however, should not replace the more traditional meetings, where thoughtful dialogue and discussion take place.

It's All About Communicating!

The residents of Grandview Estates, a low income neighborhood, were complaining about drug sales, code violations, uncut grass on vacant lots, abandoned vehicles and appliances in yards. They thought, "Maybe the city could help us get organized and do something to deal with these problems." So, they contacted City's neighborhood office.

A community meeting was held where 100 well-intentioned, civic-minded, curious neighbors to listen and to ask questions about the City's plans for the area. It was a good meeting, but afterwards rumors spread that the City was going to force residents off their land so it could develop the area with up-scale homes or high-end apartments. A second community-wide meeting was held to quell the gossip, but the talk of redevelopment continued. For months following the second meeting a small group of snipers whipped up negative sentiment about the City's motives.

After significant research, the City decided to sponsor a Saturday morning community fair so everyone could see and hear the same thing at the same time. Each department presented their current plans for the area and the timetable for accomplishing these plans. Everyone was invited and no one was excluded. All City departments set up booths and people were invited to talk one-on-one with staff, ask questions and make comments.

There were activities for the kids so parents could spend some quality time talking to their City representatives. Hotdogs, chips and soda were served. Of course, the snipers were no where to be found and the rumors were dispelled. By everyone involved, the fair was declared a big success.

Tips for Radio/ TV Call-in Talk Shows

- While fun and entertaining, it's important not to allow the "show" to overwhelm the purpose of the event.

- **Do not** put telephone callers on the air live.

- Screen questions and comments. Sanitize materials to take out personal barbs and hooks.

- Technical difficulties are always a problem.

- Call-in talk shows need to advertise well in advance to gain an audience.

- If free cable TV resources are not available, this technique has potentially high costs.

- Don't forget the radio as a vehicle for similar community engagement.

Telephone Chains

Telephone chains are much like prayer chains developed by religious groups. The purpose is to communicate important and time-critical messages quickly to specific participants in a community. For instance, if a council meeting is being held next week on a topic of special interest, then the leader would inform the five people on the first tier of the telephone chain. Those five have agreed, in advance, to call an additional five community members, each of whom have agreed, in turn, to call their five people...and so on. Like e-mail lists, telephone chains can be effective at mobilizing quick action, but take significant leadership, pre-crisis organization and the ability to gain real commitment from those early in the chain. It is possible to avoid recreating community leadership by using currently organized neighborhood groups like Block Watch who will support a broader mission. This process gets the word out, fast!

Cable TV—Taped Programs/Live Call-in Shows

Cable TV can be a real boon to community involvement if the technology is widely available. Many cities and towns have franchise agreements with the local cable TV operator to give them free access to one or more channels for use in public service. Viewers watch these public access channels at all times of the day and night, so videotapes of critical public meetings, project information and call-in shows can be viewed frequently.

Expanding the notion of cable TV as a way to conduct portions of a public involvement process is two-way, interactive cable. Yes, in some places this technology is now available, and even if two-way cable isn't in your area, you can always use the good old telephone to spice up your event.

In the past, communication was one way...from the studio to the viewer. Not only is the technology changing, but the public has become enchanted with live TV and radio call-in shows. You can use this technique to hold public hearings and town hall meetings on TV. The local telephone company can provide two or three temporary phone lines which volunteers can use to take questions and comments. Those questions and comments are then used by technical experts, policy makers, and informed guests on the show.

Community Surveys

Surveys can be very helpful in communicating with the public but can also have serious negative consequences if the tools are not well constructed. For a full discussion of the features of community surveys, see Chapter 3.

"A word means just what I intend it to mean; never more, never less!"

—Lewis Carroll
(March Hare in
Alice in Wonderland)

Ten Tips for Surviving Public Meetings

Conducting public meetings is not easy for a facilitator. The following ten tips are hard-won lessons provided to help both the experienced veteran and the rookie.

1. **The Adversarial Assumption.** People who take the time to attend public meetings are honestly concerned about the issues being discussed, and they probably would not be there if they agreed with the agency's policy direction. It is a safe bet that many of the people in the room hold an adversarial position. It is important to recognize this when you are preparing for the meeting.

2. **Understand the Environment.** If participants at a public meeting seem to treat agency representatives like "the enemy," it is probably because that is how they perceive them. These staff members assert some level of control over the participant's world. They are the collective authority of the state, and all motives are suspect.

3. **Actively Listen, Reflect Comments, Summarize Frequently.** All through the public meeting, active listening and confirmation are the best techniques for keeping the group focused and on the subject. It is important to try to understand participants' concerns and deal with their fears in a methodic but sensitive way. Frequently summarize the group's themes. For instance, "During the past five minutes, I heard you say _____. Is that accurate?"

4. **Redirect Emotional Energy.** To keep the meeting from degenerating into emotional symbolism, frequently ask the group, "How does your recommendation translate into day-to-day operation?" or "What does that mean to an

ordinary citizen?" Another way to develop effective communication with the public is to ask speakers if they can define emotionally charged words, phrases, and concepts. For instance, a participant might be asked, "Can you help me understand what you mean by ____?" This technique will also help the speaker focus on the topic at hand.

5. **Respectfully Call a Bluff.** If a participant is citing data that seems unreasonable, indicate in a respectful tone that access to such information would be helpful. "Would you provide that information and the source to all of us so everyone can review it?"

6. **No Cheap Shots!** Even if a participant is totally off base, preserve his or her dignity and self-esteem. Sarcasm, put-downs, and mockery have no place in a public meeting. Admittedly, the representative of the public agency is an easy target for participants. As a facilitator, do not respond in kind! To do so raises the emotional temperature of the meeting and makes the crowd sympathetic to the hecklers. Keep your responses focused, respectful, and controlled.

7. **Personalize the Feeling of Communication.** To overcome the "us" versus "them" mentality of public hearings, use participants' names when you address them. First names can be used if custom permits and it appears appropriate. Use first names to build a sense of familiarity, but be cautious not to make people unfamiliar with the group feel like outsiders. Although you must be careful not to overuse self-deprecating humor, it can reduce emotional distance and build rapport between the agency staff and the group.

8. **Find the Hidden Agenda as Early as Possible.** Although the meeting may be on one specific subject, the public may have something very different on their minds. People who come to these meetings usually have specific agendas and thoughts, and the longer they have to wait to say it, the angrier they become. It is important to determine early in the hearing what is on the participants' minds. Ask them to identify the issues they want to discuss. Knowing their concerns ensures they can be addressed early; reducing the negative energy they bring to the event.

9. **Keep Egos Under Control.** It is not unusual for a participant to personalize the discussion and make an unflattering comment about the agency's motives. They may do this for two reasons. First, the participant may be so scared and emotionally upset about what they perceive is being "done" to them by the agency that they lose control and lash out at any representative. These staff members are symbols of the agency. Second, the participant may want to put project managers in a defensive posture, making them appear as if they are hiding something. If staff lash back, the listeners, uncommitted community, and press may sympathize with the person baiting the speaker, thereby, weakening the agency's credibility.

10. **Keep a Sense of Humor and Admit You Are Human.** It may be helpful to simply admit that the agency does not have all the answers, but that you will work with folks to get as many as possible. When all else fails, good natured humor can be your salvation. A simple smile, a shake of the head, and shrug of the shoulders or a pregnant pause can get project staff and facilitators through a tough meeting. Above all, never lose your temper.

Things to Remember about Meetings

- Develop a detailed agenda in advance of all meetings.

- Use driving questions to focus the group's attention and energy.

- Create action plans at the end of every meeting.

- Public bodies are bound by open meeting laws.

- Assume that most participants in a public hearing will perceive the agency staff as the enemy.

- Actively listen to others and do so with an open mind.

- Help the group actively solicit and explore all minority ideas and positions.

- No cheap shots; preserve self-esteem.

- Keep your sense of humor and, when appropriate, admit that you're human.

The Ugly Face of Fear

Situation: A crowd of 4000 angry senior citizens from Sun Valley East, an age-restricted community, were gathered in a large convention auditorium to hear a developer propose a 640 acre non age-restricted subdivision on their northern border. At an open house held just prior to the hearing, people were asked to put comments and feelings on 3x5 index cards for the record, and so that speakers could focus on their specific concerns. The facilitator, George Smith, had collected 284 cards and reviewed them for themes, but one card stood out from all of rest. It would be the trump card if things got ugly.

George tried to start the meeting on time, but it was hard to get people to quiet down. The hecklers in the audience were in their glory. Each time he would ask for calm, someone would shout, "Just try to put those kids in our city!" or "Go on back to where you came from!"

Finally, George knew if the developer was to ever have a chance to present his idea, the group would have to be shamed into civility. George read a few of the cards that he'd collected before the meeting. The crowd started to listen. After each card the hecklers would start again. Finally, he came to the trump card. It read, "If we let these people into the area they'll start shopping at our stores, driving on our streets, and even attending our churches." The crowd heard those last words and the silence was deafening. Finally the pause was broken when someone in the back shouted, "That's a lie!" George went into the crowd and asked an elderly women to stand. Holding the microphone to her mouth, he asked her, "Mrs. Schmidt, would you mind reading this card?" She took the card and read it.

From that moment until the end of the hearing the crowd of 4000 was civil toward all the speakers.

Lesson: When the crowd turns ugly, use a mirror.

Chapter 7:

Managing Conflict and Mediating Community Disputes

The Story of Chicken Grove

In the audience were three different people with three very different stories to tell.

*The **Senior Citizen** really was concerned. He didn't want the fire fighters who might someday come to his aid to know he didn't want them to build the fire station in his neighborhood, but he knew how difficult it was for his wife to get to sleep with all the noise that this fire station would generate. He was also concerned about the value of his property. He and his wife would be selling their home in the next five years. He believed that if a fire station were in the area, his property values would fall.*

*The **Property Owner** didn't care who knew he was against the fire station. The town had annexed his property against his wishes, and they'd done it so quickly he hadn't had time to protest the action. He was just too happy to put a monkey wrench in any of their plans that he could. His property taxes almost doubled when the town took over. He now had police and fire protection, weekly garbage pick-up and access to central water and sewers, but he'd lived* *fine before without those things and didn't see any need to use them. He was glad he'd organized this group to protest another government boondoggle.*

*The **Neighborhood Activist** was proud to be able to participate in this civic protest. She was truly concerned about her children's safety with all those fire trucks speeding up and down the streets. She thought that a fire station would be better built ten blocks west by the commercial center where the noise and pollution from their fire trucks would not bother anyone. Why, the intrusion of a fire station into the neighborhood would look simply awful, and she intended to tell anyone who would listen what kind of monstrosity the town had planned for her neighborhood, just as soon as she was able to see the drawings of what they were planning to build.*

The Mayor called a meeting for the next day with the Town Administrator and the Fire Chief. At the meeting the Mayor asked two simple questions:

"What did we do to cause us this problem?"

"What can we do now to get back on track?"

What's wrong?

Of the fifty people demonstrating in the Town Council Chambers, we now know what's going on with three of them. But what about the other forty-seven? What motivated them to give up an evening with the TV, the family, the bowling league...and risk being labeled a whiner or nut-case to protest a fire station being built in their neighborhood? What do they want? How can the town create a forum to recognize their voices in a positive and productive way?

The tools and techniques for managing conflict and community controversy outlined in this chapter will help you conduct public discussions in a safe, civil and productive manner.

Questions to Frame Discussion:

- Why do elected officials view this decision differently than either the citizens or the town staff?

- What causes tensions within and between communities?

- Why do people disagree on fundamental values?

- Why does conflict occur?

- What techniques might agencies, communities and even individuals use to avoid conflict?

- What motivates "snipers"? How can you get "snipers" to participate in the process?

> *"Never pick a fight with someone who has nothing to lose."*
>
> Lindworth's Fourth Principle of Survival

Let's Talk about Snipers

Ever heard the term "sniper" used to describe someone outside the circle of agreement on a public discussion? If not, then let's define these folks and describe how and why they operate the way they do. The term will be used frequently from this point on in the workbook.

"Snipers" come in two varieties. The first type can be good for the community involvement process. They've been left out of the discussions of changes that will impact their lives. They want a voice and some sense of control over their future. If the Town is smart, they will apologize sincerely for overlooking the "snipers" in this matter, set a place at the table, and invite them into the process. These folks will bring their fears and concerns, their ideas and intellectual energy to the discussion. They will work toward an understanding of the situation that prompted the proposed change, and they will help you find ways to shape the decision so that they can support it. In the long run these "snipers" will become contributors. They will serve as civic leaders, sit on boards and commissions, and may even become elected officials, themselves. Enlightened self-interest? Maybe, but they took the time to get involved. The community benefits from that involvement.

The second type of "sniper" is another flavor altogether. Their interests may not be so pure as the first and they certainly are not interested in the kind of problem solving you're promoting. These "snipers" do not raise their voices to contribute to the discussion of a solution. Their interest is in arguing, disputing, challenging, criticizing and opposing whatever is being proposed. The process of public involvement provides them with a platform to gain attention. They stimulate continued dissent but not in the name of problem solving. They gain more from the process when problems remain unsolved. Their interests lie in promoting controversy.

Having said all that, you might think that these "snipers" are terrible people. In fact, some our most revered political and civil rights leaders fall into this category of "sniper." When leaders find social conditions that clearly indicate broad change is required they may become "snipers." "Snipers" use these examples of injustice as mirrors to reflect, focus and intensify the need for change. If issues are resolved too quickly these "snipers" lose the opportunity for more comprehensive gains. For instance, had the Rev. Martin Luther King, Jr. brought the garbage workers in Memphis to the bargaining table without a strike in 1966, they might have been able to negotiate the improved working conditions that were being requested. Had he extracted a pay increase or some added benefits the opportunity to showcase injustice to a national audience might have evaporated. There were larger issues at hand, and Dr. King used the sanitation strike to highlight them.

If Rosa Parks had not continued "sniping" during the 382 days of the Montgomery bus strike, would we still have segregation? Had Caesar Chavez incrementally resolved the demands of farm laborers in the southwest, would reform have ever come for migrant workers? Never dismiss a "sniper" as just another angry person with too much time on their hands. Listen hard because they may have something you can learn and use. A form is included in the Appendix called a "Sniper Plan" that will help you organize your thinking and develop strategies for coping with these unique individuals when they arrive.

"The end move in politics is always to pick up a gun."

—Buckminster Fuller

Conflict in a Community Involvement Setting

The anger, fear and resentment illustrated in the Chicken Grove story is very common to community involvement processes. Headlines in newspapers announce that almost any decision made by public officials adversely affects someone in the community. By definition, the work of government is beneficial to the citizens. If it weren't helpful the people would revolt and "throw the rascals out." The poorly performing mayor and council would be replaced with people who would do the right things. Occasionally a council, commission or legislature will be completely dismissed, but not frequently.

Why would anyone want to become an elected official? The job requires constant research, training and study. The pay is lousy. When you do something good the people figure that's just your job...nothing special. In fact, constituents rarely say thank you. But just wait to make an honest mistake. The voters tan your hide and hang it on the wall as part of the next election. Most of the time you suffer, and your family and friends suffer by affiliation. And for all this misery you have the honor, every two to four years, of asking these ungrateful people to please give you another chance to serve them. It ain't much of a job, but those who can put up with the bad stuff in order to do the good stuff deserve our respect and admiration.

Likewise for the people who run the bureaucracy. They're the ones who build and maintain your streets, roads and bridges. They inspect your homes whether you want them to or not. They provide fire protection and emergency medical assistance. They enforce your laws...even the speed limits you don't like. They educate your kids, pick up your garbage, make sure that when you turn on the faucet that clean, safe water comes out, and when you flush the toilet all that nasty stuff goes someplace other than the bathroom floor. These are the public employees who make America great, and do it on a budget that you can afford. And yes, they're also the ones who send you tax bills and manage your money.

It's obvious to most citizens that our public servants are doing a good job, overall. The decisions they're making are, in their opinion, in the best interest of the entire community they serve. Unfortunately, some constituents may feel that providing public services is contrary to their personal or collective interests. The contractor who's required to replace a house foundation because it doesn't meet the building code is understandably unhappy with the service that the inspector provided. The guy driving 30 miles per hour over the speed limit isn't particularly pleased when the motorcycle cop issues him a ticket. The woman who shows up at the library on Monday evening only to find out that it closed at 6:00 pm due to lack of funds wants to know why her needs are given second priority to a sewer plant expansion. And everyone is upset when they get their property tax bill and it's been increased by $100 to pay for a new school. These are examples of public services that most of us strongly support...until we become affected personally.

These are the decisions that elected officials and staff must make to keep our towns, cities, counties and states running smoothly, but they always seem to create controversy. You'd think by this time that the people would have learned that there is no free lunch, so get over it! But that's not the case, nor should it be the case. Proposing a new wastewater treatment plant or landfill will always get the attention of the people living in the surrounding area. Building freeways is a real boon to the traveling public, but a bane to the people living within the alignment who have to move. Worse yet, there are people now living right next to the

> "How will that decision affect me? If it hurts my position, then I'm against it! If it isn't in my best interest...then I'm probably against it, too. If it causes me to change anything, I'm definitely against it. Of course, if it gives me a financial or personal advantage... if I can see a direct personal benefit...then I may support it."
>
> "Now, tell me again. How good will it be if I support it?"

freeway who won't be relocated and are stuck with increased air pollution, traffic and noise. Even something as positive as a park can create friction within a neighborhood and headaches for policy makers. "Whatdaya, mean you're going to put lights at the ball diamonds! My house sits across from those fields. The noise alone will drive me crazy."

A Framework for Approaching Community Conflict

So as we approach managing conflict and controversy, let's all acknowledge that:

- As our society becomes faster paced and gets more complicated, the problems we face will become more complicated. There are few simple solutions that will satisfy everyone's needs.

- All conflict and controversy centers around change. You want someone else to change. They want you to change. You both want the government to change. The government wants you to change. Think about it.

- People have opinions. When you ask them to change they want the chance to voice an opinion and be sure it's heard.

- People have the right to truthful, accurate, timely and meaningful information about issues that affect them.

- No one likes to change, but it's usually easier to take if it's your own decision.

- Change is easier to accommodate when it's still a long way off.

- As human beings, we still don't communicate very well, but we can improve if we try really hard.

By using these seven points to help people involved in public controversy communicate, they will find ways to make change work to their advantage.

At the root of public disputes are conflicts in core values. These conflicts are buried deep, but they drive feelings and behaviors. During the public involvement process people are frequently forced to confront how the changes being proposed will align with their values. To understand the core of a dispute, participants must disclose their values, beliefs and feelings about the topic. As they do, they must also contend with how implementing change based on those beliefs will affect others within their community. Sound complicated? Not really. Let's take an example:

> *Mr. Jones has two children with the potential to be world-class swimmers. He believes that the town needs a new Olympic-sized swimming pool to help his and other kids sharpen their aquatic skills. He's worked hard to make his dream bear fruit. He created a "Build the Swimming Pool" bond committee, and he got his wish. The voters approved the money to build a pool. But the town policy makers learned the only place a pool that size could be built is in the middle of a declining neighborhood. To do this the town will have to acquire and demolish 50 low-income rental homes.*
>
> *Mrs. Smith lives in one of those homes and doesn't want to move. She's created a "People not Pools" neighborhood committee and is fighting to have the idea of a pool abandoned.*
>
> *Mr. Jones wants a pool. If he is successful in promoting his values that would build a pool, then Mrs. Smith will have to move. This action would be counter to her values that say she should be able to live where she now resides. If*

Mrs. Smith successfully maintains her values and is successful in defeating the pool construction, then Mr. Jones' dream is crushed. His values are not sustained.

Who's right? Who's wrong? Whose values should prevail?

To understand what is "at" issue both Mr. Jones and Mrs. Smith must communicate the reasons they hold their opinions. This means they must articulate what they believe is right, and what values they promote. Once this communication occurs, then both parties can make one of three decisions. Each could be true to their own values and continue the fight until one wins and other loses. One could concede their position to assure that the other is able to achieve their dream. As a third option, they might work together to find creative ways to sustain both values simultaneously.

Within a community involvement process participants must first bring their real concerns to full public disclosure. Hiding feelings and beliefs behind a sham of academic discourse, analytic debate, and political correctness just extends the conflict. During a recent engagement the discussion centered on the number of motor vehicles passing through an intersection daily. Was there a need for a traffic light, or would a traffic sign do just as well. Neighbors politely debated whether the traffic count was accurate. All of a sudden a mother of four children jumped up and shouted to the group, "I don't give a darn about the number of cars going through there. It only takes one to kill one of my kids." Later it was learned that people opposing the traffic light believed that such an action would reduce the value of their homes adjacent to the corner. Once the real values, beliefs and feelings were disclosed, the group was able to make progress and send a unified recommendation to the city streets and traffic commission.

"The" Issue versus "At" Issue

The critical question is not, "What is the issue" but rather, "What is at issue?" There is more than a semantic distinction here. "The" issue often hides behind socially acceptable excuses and conventional wisdom. "At" issue has the raw underpinnings of human emotion. For example, two of "the" issues neighborhoods fighting racial integration used during the 1950's and 1960's were 1) protecting the right of people to live with whom they choose, and 2) Biblical references to God's instruction that all things live among their own kind. Both of these statements were socially acceptable to most people at that time. Stating either of these positions avoided being crude, blunt and outright offensive. What was "at" issue were deep-seated feelings of 1) inbred racial hatred, 2) the fear that integration would mean a loss of property values, and 3) possible loss of exclusive political and social power. "The" issues were politically correct for the time, and what was "at" issue was ugly, crude and not acceptable for polite company. We still use many of these same euphemistic conventions to avoid honest discussions of public issues.

If you haven't figured this out yet, the community involvement process being promoted in this workbook actually solicits conflict and controversy by forcing disclosure and confrontation. The objective is to manage fear and anger in a safe, civil, socially acceptable, and democratic way. The person responsible for the public involvement process becomes a facilitator of the group's discussion. The facilitator is charged with helping communities resolve controversy.

> "The Issue" is a point, matter or dispute, the decision of which is of public importance. When referring to "The Issue" it can be defined as a trend or event that can have an important influence on the community's ability to reach its desired future.
>
> "At Issue" refers to the individual foundation elements comprising the dispute. .. the overall issue. "What really is at issue is..."

Defining the Facilitator's Role

A facilitator is a guide, who takes a group to a predetermined place in a predetermined length of time. The predetermined place is an answer to a specific driving question. Do not confuse "an answer" with "the answer." "The answer" is of no consequence to a facilitator, but "an answer" is.

A facilitator is not a teacher, trainer, instructor, or mentor. A facilitator is a guide who helps the group cross a series of barriers, and moves them toward an answer to a driving question. During this journey, the facilitator assures all participants certain privileges and rights, and in return, retains a significant amount of authority and power over the process. A facilitator is a neutral servant of the group who uses active listening as a primary skill. A facilitator does not evaluate but protects individuals from criticism and abuse, encourages broad participation, senses group dynamics and moods, keeps the process on track and on time, plans and executes meeting logistics, and then summarizes what is said. Above all else, the facilitator is bound by process and does not provide any substantive content to the discussion.

Managing Unproductive and Destructive Conflict

If groups hope to reach substantial agreement on public issues, they must first agree to open themselves to honest communication. An honest discussion, whether inside or outside of a formal meeting, will probably generate controversy. To manage the conflict and make the effort a constructive exercise, the group must subscribe to some fundamental ground rules within which the facilitator can work. This means negotiating an agreement with all participants at the very beginning of a process on the behaviors that will and will not be acceptable to the group.

- **Honesty, Candor and Confidentiality:** Within this process how safe is it to be honest? Can I say the things that need to be said, or do I have to mask them in politically correct terms? What signals will you give me before you say something shocking? What can we do to keep honest feelings and comments from becoming embarrassing sound bytes in the newspaper?

- **Straightforward Communication:** If we have positions on issues, we'll share them. If we change our minds, we'll let everyone know as soon as possible. If we don't have a position...then we'll say that, too. We will ask only honest questions and try to make only clear comments.

- **Active Listening:** Listening has been defined as "the time spent waiting until it's your turn to talk." We all agree to use active listening skills. By doing so, we can avoid misunderstandings. If we don't understand something we will ask for clarification. We will repeat what we heard before we disagree on it.

- **Personal Respect:** We agree to critique ideas, not people. We will show respect for the views of others. Before speaking or acting, we will check our assumptions and determine what collateral effect those words or actions might have on our working relationships. When others are speaking, we will listen and avoid side conversations.

- **No surprises!!!**

- **Focus on the Future:** What happened in the past, stays in the past. From today on, we agree to move forward for the good of the community and its future.

- **Facilitator's Role:** We will use the facilitator as a sounding board to test ideas and discuss difficulties.

- **Honor Limited Time:** Everyone is responsible for advancing our agenda and we have limited time to get our work done. To make the most of that time, we agree to use a "thirty-second soapbox" format for our meetings.

- **Make Good Decisions:** Our job is to develop the best alternatives and make the best decisions we can. We will open our minds and hearts to finding the best resolution possible. In this manner, we will plan for action.

- **Enjoy the Journey:** We will invest significant time toward this effort. To the best of our ability, we will enjoy our time together.

- **Functional, Constructive Controversy:** There will be controversy in all we do. When we're done, we will have grown out of the controversy toward some resolution. Whatever we do, we will make it functional and productive.

Consensus-based Decisions

Consensus, consent, grudging consent, majority rule are all terms used to discuss how a group will know when they are in substantial agreement on an issue. Voting and the majority rule that usually goes with it, mean some participants win while other participants lose. Voting is not a good way to obtain long-term commitment and agreement and most community involvement processes avoid voting at all costs. The other techniques depend on some level of compromise or creative thinking to find more inclusive solutions. Short of unanimity, the standard of quality for group agreement is consensus.

The term "consensus" is used frequently by facilitators to describe the lowest level of acceptable agreement by a group that results in proceeding with action on a controversial issue. The features of consensus include 1) agreement that addresses the central issues but may not address every concern or be perfect from every possible perspective, 2) agreement to full or limited support for a period of time, and 3) a commitment to not actively undermine the decision.

- Consensus means taking the time to find an optimal resolution to an issue. Consensus is reached when most of the participants like the alternative, and everyone else agrees to abide by the alternative even though they may not believe it is the best way to go.

- Consensus takes more time in the initial stages of decision making, but saves time in implementation.

- An apparent impasse can be handled when a good facilitator knows when to say "we've brought this issue as close as we can to resolution at this point in our history." Stalemate is always a possibility.

- A good facilitator knows there is no final solution to public issues. Given the state of any issue at any particular time, temporary resolution is about the best that can be reached. When conditions change, so do the outcomes of the issue resolution process. Each time the environment of the issue changes, the definition of the issue changes.

Consensus is a time-consuming but highly effective method used by groups to make decisions that last. It is a result of communication that has been open and a group climate that has been supportive enough so everyone in the group feels he or she has had a fair chance to influence the decision (see definitions in Chapter 1). Consensus is neither a vote where majority rules nor total agreement. Consensus is not a quick way to make decisions and is inappropriate for crisis decisions.

Why is consensus effective?

Consensus-based decision making provides equal opportunity for everyone to influence the outcome of a decision. Every person has the same amount of power and potential to affect the outcome by finding new solutions and common ground through discussions. By encouraging participants to find unique solutions that respect the collective wisdom and multiple alternatives, a consensus is more likely to create "win-win" solutions. Agreement is reached without a vote and reinforces collaborative decision processes. When everyone understands why a decision was made, implementation of the decision is easier. Including implementers in decision making develops ownership of the process and encourages long-term commitment to the decision.

The following are thoughts and processes that might be used to bring a group to closure and/or agreement.

Consensus-seeking Behavior

Here are some ways you can create consensus-seeking behavior during meetings.

- Actively solicit and explore all minority ideas and positions before deciding.

- Establish clear discussion boundaries and issue statements before beginning.

- Acquire and thoroughly analyze all relevant data.

- Listen to the ideas of others with an open mind.

- Help others clarify and develop their own points of view.

- Make every alternative as strong as possible.

- After discussion and modification, let ideas belong to the group.

- Offer criticism only after significant discussion of an idea.

- Consider alternatives objectively and on the basis of the intended result.

- Don't over-generalize disagreement. Be specific on what a disagreement constitutes.

- Freely express any reservations.

- Restate the decision, idea or approach prior to adoption; avoid later confusion.

Only two meetings I've held in 25 years ever started to turn physically violent.

The first one was a public hearing sponsored by a state agency to discuss poisoning a small lake. The action was suggested to eliminate a specific predatory fish from the eco-system. There was an increasingly belligerent tone by a small group of men who continued to enter and exit the facility (a barn at the county fairground). It wasn't until I physically wandered into the middle of the group that I realized that one of the "anti" people had a keg of beer in the back of his pick-up truck.

Physical violence was threatened at another meeting where you normally wouldn't expect it. In this relatively upscale, college community where everyone is usually polite and proper, the subject of the meeting was the provocative element: Youth baseball!!!

Managing Conflict in Meetings

Holding well-designed and properly structured meetings goes a long way to minimizing unproductive community conflict. A poorly designed meeting is a pressure cooker that has no way to release steam. If an experienced facilitator is not actively managing the event, things can quickly get ugly and may even turn violent.

Actions a facilitator must take to prepare for an event lay the foundation for civil dialogue. Many of these activities were outlined in detail in Chapter 6, but are worth repeating in summary.

- Develop a written agenda and a written set of meeting objectives prior to the meeting. Distribute these materials to potential participants in advance to start building positive and accurate expectations.

- Determine how much time to allot to each part of the meeting. Within reason and the open meeting laws, give the participants permission to make minor revisions to the agenda to address their concerns. Remind participants of the time allotted for each item as they initiate discussion, and at appropriate times during the discussion.

- Prepare driving questions that help the group frame the discussion.

- Frequently probe for substantive understanding of key issues. Ask the group how they might summarize the comments. Ask individuals to not only state their own positions but also the positions of those they oppose.

- Plan the logistics of the meeting to avoid technical difficulties. Assure that the group can focus on the substance of the discussion, and not the temperature of the room, poor audio-visual devices, unacceptable restrooms or the noisy group in the room next door.

- Make all participants feel safe and comfortable. If even one voice is not heard because of fear from reprisal by either the agency or other participants, then the process has failed.

The Rookie and the Microphone

Situation: The professional meeting facilitator that the town had hired to run a public hearing had three associates working the floor with wireless microphones. Two of these associates had worked public hearings before and knew what to expect, but the third was a rookie. As the public comment portion of the meeting proceeded, people were asked to stand, state their name and make a 30-second comment highlighting their feelings on the issues at hand. The idea was to provide the town council with a balanced perspective and avoiding a situation where one person or group dominates the presentation.

Everything was civil until the rookie associate released his wireless microphone to the "no-growth" opposition leader. The leader made his comment and then handed it to another member of his group, who proceeded to give it to another member of the group, ad infinitum. It was 20 minutes before the rookie was able to retrieve the microphone. Needless to say, the balance that the town desired wasn't achieved.

Lesson: "Never give up the mic!!! Hold on like it's your last breath of air."

Tips for Holding Personal Conversations

- Use personal conversation to understand; really listen and understand what people are telling you.

- Take the initiative; don't wait for people to come to you.

- Don't call people in to talks; go to them.

- Be sure to talk with those whom you feel will be the strongest opponents; you need to understand their perspective most of all.

- Talk with food; make it friendly and social.

Keeping Out of Trouble

During a controversial meeting the facilitator will occasionally have to deal with personal confrontation, polarization, and even "group think". The facilitator must not let the twists and turns of group dynamics affect the group's performance. People within groups will behave in predictable ways, and with experience the facilitator can start to anticipate that behavior. The greater the experience and more skillful the facilitator, the easier will be the job of managing the meeting.

The following are group and interpersonal techniques used by facilitators to help groups maintain civility but make progress during a discussion.

- Be friendly, patient, sensitive during a discussion session, but, maintain a thick skin to endure the personal attacks that are sure to come.

- Use humor to defuse personal confrontations.

- Don't be afraid to be aggressive, but always be polite and never rude when confronting individuals.

- Find experts in the group and draw on them as content sources when appropriate to the topic, but don't allow experts to dominate the discussion.

- Trust the process and stick to the script, especially when things are not going as you expected.

- Use silence and the "pregnant pause" to press the group when a difficult or sensitive issue is being discussed.

- Empower the group to take responsibility and claim success.

- Solicit personal illustrations and stories to clarify points, where appropriate.

- Use reflective listening and humor to overcome stress, anger and hostility.

- Acknowledge contributions by repeating the point, when appropriate.

- Use eye contact and body language to tell the participant, "I'm listening and care about what you're saying."

- Provide a shunt for the group's aggression.

- Absorb and redirect destructive anger and hostility.

- Protect individual participants, make conflict constructive and helpful to the group.

- Do not take anger personally.

- Play "devil's advocate" when the group is coming to consensus too easily.

- Actively solicit help from the participants when questions are raised.

- Trust the group. If the group has the right information and sufficient time, they will do the "right" thing and make appropriate choices.

- Make individual participants feel valued.

- Remain neutral, frequently pause to give people time to think and reflect, ask subordinate, detailed questions to probe for more detail, encourage participation, and manage digression and dominance.

- Keep on time.

Tips for Holding Personal Conversations

- Hang out with people; visit popular local gathering places and ask people what they think about the issue or problem and the process.

- Don't be defensive.

- Be trustworthy; build a relationship; invite people to keep participating.

- Caution: don't use personal conversation to cut deals and violate an agreed-to public process.

- Use conversations throughout any process you design; sometimes, personal conversations are all that's necessary to achieve agreement.

- Frequently ask the group, "Are we moving toward closure?"

- Determine the tensions that keep the stakeholders from agreeing once the issue has been defined.

- Describe the field of tensions and the paradox that exist.

- Remove your ego from the discussion.

- Challenge the process and not the motives.

- Develop a central driving question in conjunction with the meeting and put it in writing.

- Find the hidden agenda by looking for it in advance.

- Include the "unlisted agenda", team building, in the process.

- Keep a clear understanding of the facilitator's role, the group's role and the driving questions.

- Make sure everyone has an opportunity to participate and contribute to the discussion.

- Ask permission when in doubt.

Group Mediation as an Alternative to Typical Facilitation

Mediation is often thought to be a process related to but distinct from typical group facilitation. Where facilitation emphasizes orderly, but free-flowing discussion about an issue, the focus of mediation is to resolve conflict and find a point of agreement where both sides can be satisfied. Mediation is appropriate when conflict is significant and approaching the boiling point. Defusing the atmosphere may be a necessary preamble to facilitating a solution. In mediation there is a formal process to be followed and rules are strict. While typical mediation offers two private parties in dispute an opportunity to resolve specific issues between them, mediation techniques can be adapted for multiple-stakeholder, public policy discussions, too.

Ground Rules for Mediation Sessions

Before beginning a mediation session, the parties should agree, in writing, to the following terms and conditions:

- No shouting, name calling, or putting down one another.

- Discuss issues openly and honestly.

- Express anger in a constructive, non-blame assessing language.

- No physical violence.

- Listen to each other as carefully as possible and do not interrupt. If an issue arises while one party is speaking, the other party can write a reminder note to address the issue at a later time.

- Treat each other with respect.

- The mediators agree to conduct themselves in the following manner:

  - They will not judge the parties.

  - They will be neutral.

  - They will facilitate the mediation process.

  - They will keep information learned in the mediation confidential unless disclosure is mandated by law or requested and agreed upon in writing by both parties.

Impasse Strategies

The term "impasse" refers to a deadlock where no further progress toward agreement can be made. Impasse means stalemate, standstill, and cessation of discussions or a point where two or more parties will no longer search for agreement. During any mediation process, the facilitator may discover that there are points or specific issues where the parties refuse to negotiate any further. The following is a process that can help you move a group past impasse.

Steps in Resolving Impasse

1. Identify an impasse has occurred. State that it appears the parties are no longer making progress or willing to search for an answer.

2. Review and highlight any progress previously made and describe the "here's where we are" conditions. "Here's what you wanted...and here's what you were willing to give up." If possible, make a polarity diagram that shows disputants where they were when they started and where they are currently.

3. State to the parties in dispute that they have options other than continuing the discussions, but there are also consequences of failing to reach a mediated settlement. Do not breach the confidences of either party when giving information about alternatives.

4. Ask all parties if they are still committed to working toward an agreement. Keep in mind that as a mediator, you have no responsibility for keeping them in discussions or assuring their success, but are a neutral third party aiding the disputants in the mediation process.

Techniques for Breaking an Impasse

The Caucus

- Separate the disputants.

- Privately ask them what they saw going on during the mediation.

- Tell them what you saw.

- Review their "wants" to look for hidden agendas.

- Review the benefits and consequences of reaching a settlement.

- Explore what they are "willing" to give up.

- Explore any face-saving ideas that might aid in discussions.

The Line

- Draw a horizontal line to demonstrate where both parties began, where they are now and who is moving and who is not. This strategy is particularly good for resolving quantitative issues like money, time, etc.

Brainstorming

- Stop the process and ask everyone involved in the discussions to brainstorm alternatives.

- Set a time limit for discussions.

- Using a white board, flip chart or storyboard, write down all ideas that are presented.

- Remind participants that 1) they should strive for as many suggestions as they can think of, 2) all ideas are welcome, and 3) no judgments about the quality of any suggestion.

- Stop brainstorming.

- Ask participants "What suggestions appeal to you on this list?"

- Return to the "willing to do".

Role-Reversal

- Ask parties to stand up and (physically) exchange places...to sit in the other person's chair...and to put themselves in the other person's situation.

- In order, ask each party how they feel and what they want (being the other person). If the report is incomplete or inaccurate, help the person state what they want, or remember some relevant fact that they may have missed.

- When all parties are finished and you feel mutual understanding has been achieved, ask the disputants to return to their original seats. Thank them for doing the exercise.

- See if there is anything that they are now willing to do, since they understand the other person's position better.

The One-Down Technique

- Tell the disputants that you have no more ideas to help them, but because of their demonstrated commitment to the process, you do not want to see the mediation fail.

- Ask the disputants if they see any way progress might be made to keep settlement discussions alive.

- Seek the disputants' help as a way to help the mediation and you as the mediator to succeed in reaching resolution.

The Incremental Proposal Process

- Party #1 submits a proposal.

- Ask Party #2 if they understand the proposal (not whether they agree with it).

- Ask Party #2 if they have any problems with the proposal, and if so, to identify what is causing them concern.

- Ask Party #1 if they understand the problems that Party #2 has (not whether they agree with it).

- Ask Party #2 to submit a proposal (counterproposal) that would address the situation <u>and</u> take care of the problems they had with Party #1's proposal.

- Ask Party #1 if they understand the proposal (not whether they agree with it).

- Ask Party #1 if they have any problems with the proposal, and if so, to identify what is causing them concern.

- Ask Party #2 if they understand Party #1's concerns.

- Continue in this manner until all concerns are addressed within the framework of a proposed solution.

Things to Remember

- While moving toward an answer to the problems facing the group, caution is needed if the answer appears to be a clear reflection of some canned thinking. (Canned thinking is a pre-packaged solution brought to the meeting by one or more of the participants.) Careful listening, considered thought, and perhaps some arguing should be used to generate answers. The group should be challenged to work hard and find their own, unique answers.

- The facilitator needs to be familiar with and committed to the agenda, and willing to follow the "game" plan. At the same time be ready to change the approach if the group believes it is in their best interest to do so.

- There is great benefit from just discussing the topic, and often the discussion process is more valuable than the recommendations developed.

- The facilitator needs to be enthusiastic about the process, and use that enthusiasm to gauge the needs of the group and keep them on track. If they need a boost...give it to them. If they're too playful and need to settle down, use your voice and body to send the message that it's time to get serious.

- Listening is the most important skill of the facilitator.

- The best resolution to an issue may be found in an unlikely place. Look for unique opportunities and "out-of-the-box" options. Don't let obvious alternatives and conventional wisdom set the boundaries for the discussion.

Chapter 8:
Capacity Building...Preparing for the Future

The Story of Chicken Grove

It was the day after Chief Harry's meeting with the mayor and the town manager about the riot that occurred in the Town Council Chambers. Harry looked around his office and thought, "Man, have things changed since I was a rookie pulling fire hose and washing trucks." Harry had come up through the ranks, and all his previous fire chiefs had been "take control" guys who just wouldn't have allowed citizens to protest over a new fire station. He wasn't exactly sure why all this happened and he didn't really know what to do next, but he knew that the mayor and manager were counting on him to make things right. So, as every good fire chief does when confronting crisis and unfamiliar territory, Harry told his new deputy chief to figure it out and bring him a solution.

Deputy Chief John Johnson had been watching from the "cheap seats" as the fire station controversy unfolded. When he got the call from the Chief, John knew he was going to earn his salary on this one. He had most recently worked for a large, urban city where public controversy was common fare. Deputy John had faced angry citizens on several occasions and didn't like the thought

of having to do so again, but Chief Harry was no fool. He knew John was up to the task.

It was Monday morning, the start of a new week and the beginning of Chicken Grove's new community involvement program. John took the previous weekend to analyze the past two months of work surrounding the fire station project. He embarked on a one-man program assessment and found that the town did a pretty good job of assessing community fire needs, property options and response times, but had almost no data on the demographics and social issues of the area. Further, he noted that there were at least five alternative station sites that could serve Chicken Grove's needs almost as well as the one being proposed. Why hadn't the Committee considered the options?

At 10:00 am the staff planning team assembled in the conference room. Included in the discussion was Planner Sue who was still fuming over recent citizen opposition to her proposal, Budgeter Bill the department's financial analyst, and Builder Brenda the capital improvements manager. Being an enlightened, new-millennium kind of guy he first asked the team to describe, in unemotional terms, what had occurred during the process. He was amazed at how intuitive Bill and Brenda were in recognizing the mistakes the Town had made. They listed the lack of discussions with the immediate neighbors prior to selecting the site as the biggest error. They also noted that the other possible station sites had not been fully explored with the Committee and that information on future growth was limited to the next five years.

Planner Sue sat quietly with her arms crossed as they discussed her project. She thought, "Here sit the Monday morning quarterbacks...the Johnny-come-lately's eager to criticize. Where were they when this project got started?"

Harry noticed Sue's mood and drew her into the conversation by asking, "Sue, you've been closer to this than any of us. If you had the chance to do it all over again, what would you do differently?" Sue was surprised at John's question. Because of last week's public relations disaster she expected him to lay a guilt trip and lots of blame at her feet, but he didn't.

"Well," she replied. "The first thing I'd do is throw everything out that I've ever learned in building the previous four fire stations."

Everyone laughed, so John's question broke the ice.

"Then I guess it's time," John said, "to start over. Beginning today, Chicken Grove will take a new approach...a new strategy when we build fire stations in the future."

The group was now ready for the next round of community involvement.

What's wrong?

Absolutely nothing! Every community has to start somewhere on the road to public involvement. It isn't until an agency has a blow out that they take the time to ask if there is a better, fairer, more effective way to manage the decision process.

Could Chief Harry have the skills to help Chicken Grove move to the new model? Probably not. Harry was trapped in what he thought was the "right way" to build fire stations.

Can Chief Harry learn, grow and adopt these new ways? Sure. When he sees the positive response and benefits of involving community people in the decision process he may accept John's new methods. Unfortunately, Harry is still worried about "giving the keys to the institution to the inmates." Harry might ask John, "What happens if they learn too much about our day-to-day operations? There is such a thing as too much information!"

Did it take someone outside the normal department system to raise these issues? Absolutely! And it isn't Deputy John that is the hero of the day. It was the community residents who, in their protest to the town council, stated, "This isn't right and we want to be involved."

Questions to Frame Discussion:

- What did Deputy John do to start the healing process with his staff?

- What did the Fire Department do right the first time through the process?

- What can the Fire Department do differently next time to get a better outcome from their community involvement?

- How might the Fire Department document its progress?

- What can the Town of Chicken Grove do to institutionalize the community involvement process and build civic collaboration?

Civic Collaboration

Our job as facilitators of community involvement is to provide safe places and civil ways to discuss controversial issues. In doing so, we build the ethic of community collaboration and make the job of government easier and more effective. But civic collaboration is not just about doing great research or holding exquisite meetings. It's also about building trust in public processes and the people who manage those processes. To build that trust, agency staff must honestly analyze their own work, always looking for better, more effective ways to do the public's business. It requires planning and patience to communicate with the broader community, including the news media, about civic collaboration. All this means that citizens and residents, staff, policy makers, and a variety of institutional actors all need to be educated about the requirements of a healthy community involvement process.

In November 1995 Scott London published an article for the Pew Partnership for Civic Change called "Collaboration and Community." In this article he defines civic collaboration as "a process of shared decision making in which all the parties with a stake in a problem constructively explore their differences and develop a joint strategy for action. The ethic of collaboration is premised on the belief that politics does not have to be a zero-sum game where one party wins and one party loses, or where both sides settle for a compromise. If the right people are brought together in constructive ways and with the appropriate information they can not only create authentic visions and strategies for addressing their joint problems but also, in many cases, overcome their limited perspectives of what is possible."

All of us engaged in resolving public controversy need to keep Mr. London's view of civic collaboration in mind, always.

The Project Autopsy

The final stage of community involvement is post-process analysis. This is often ignored by agency staff who, after completing a public involvement process, are just bone tired. Once the final report and meeting documentation is submitted to the city clerk or county recorder for permanent storage, people just want to get back to "business as usual." But they never can.

The memory of a community involvement process, successful or unsuccessful, will keep staff constantly on alert for situations requiring public input in the future. Agency staff experienced in the process will understand the power of community involvement. Those staff who did not participate need instruction. Future projects can benefit from analysis, and the project autopsy is a method for disassembling the previous work, giving staff the time to debrief and reflect.

A project autopsy is really quite simple:

- When the project is finished, the primary sponsor, the agency staff supporting the process, and even some of the community participants should gather for about two hours to celebrate completion.

- One person acts as a facilitator and asks the questions—
  - Were the outcomes and objectives achieved? If so, why? If not, why not?
  - What did we do right?
  - What was done wrong?
  - What were the unintended benefits or problems?
  - What, if we did it again, would we change?

Community Involvement Acronyms

NIMBY = Not In My Back Yard!

NOPE = Not On Planet Earth!

NUMA = Not Under My Administration!

BANANA = Build Absolutely Nothing Anywhere Near Anything!

CAVE = Citizens Against Virtually Everything

LULU = Locally Undesirable Land Uses

POPO = Point Of Personal Opinion

- From this meeting project staff need to record their answers and submit one final report—a report to themselves.

The autopsy report should contain a complete outline of all the steps they took during the community involvement process, the meeting agendas with summary minutes, a list of participants, the research findings, and any other substantive documents generated.

The autopsy report is to the original community involvement plan what the "as built" drawings are to the original architect's specifications.

As future community involvement projects are brought forward. staff can recount the steps taken during earlier events. They can anticipate the problems that occurred and the tactics that failed. The list of participants from a previous project can be the starting point for finding potential community mediators.

Educating Agency Staff

The staff who were actively involved in a community involvement process are probably already aware of the step-by-step activities that were part of the program. (If not, it may be helpful to expose agency staff to the fundamental underpinnings of community involvement theory by asking them to read this book.) Staff who were not part of the process are probably wondering what was happening during those long night meetings with the angry mobs. Undoubtedly, there were lots of agency reports and probably some newspaper stories generated by the process. To those who are uninitiated the question may be looming, "Why was the agency taking all this time and money, and delaying important decisions, just to talk to the public?"

Educating Elected and Appointed Policy Makers

Another important group to educate about community involvement is the policy makers who patiently waited outside the discussions until the community involvement process was completed. This group includes elected officials, appointed board members and commissioners, and top agency managers. They may be able to see the ultimate benefit of the process, but may not understand why it works. If policy makers are left uninformed, they can become barriers to future public involvement.

Barriers to Sponsoring and Participating in a Community Involvement Process

Below are listed some anticipated barriers common to community involvement. It is important to note why these obstacles exist, and some of the ways to avoid them over time.

- **Fear of criticism.** This feeling is universal. Internally, staff may feel threatened by people knowing just a little about what is happening within the organization. If they don't know the "why" of the activity, there is a risk of questions and criticism. "If we just keep our cards close enough to our chest, we can get this done and no one will even know the difference. If we let folks know too much too early...the project can be halted."

  Elected officials also suffer from fear of criticism. Participants who feel they are on the losing end of a controversy could claim that elected officials lack courage. "You're giving the decision to these trouble-makers because you don't have the guts to make it yourself!" Being called a coward doesn't feel good to anyone, and participating in a public involvement process could be seen as a sign of weakness rather than patience and strength of character.

> *When confronting options that are unanimously unacceptable or offensive to the group members, it's amazing how quickly the group can find an acceptable universe of alternatives.*
>
> Lindworth's
> Fifth Law of Consensus

Fear of criticism is not isolated to just agency actors. Community and stakeholder group leaders can be charged by their own constituents with "selling out" to the government, or lacking sufficient mettle for a real, knock-down fight with the bureaucracy.

- **Fear of failure.** Most agency actors and stakeholder participants want to succeed in the community involvement process. When a group fails to reach substantive agreement there is a stigma placed on both the individuals who participated and the process. Sensing possible failure, support for a group's work could dwindle. Community leaders representing stakeholder groups may distance themselves from the process. A public meeting or event can go poorly and policy-maker support can quickly disappear.

- **Unbalanced power.** When one party's voice in a dispute becomes so unusually strong that legitimate minority opinions cannot be heard, then it is the responsibility of the process facilitator to balance the discussion. Community involvement can be labeled as unfair by one position because it views another group as having too much power or influence over the process.

- **Fear of losing control.** Agency staff may feel that, as professionals in their fields, they know best how to assess and address problems. When outsiders are brought into the discussion the insiders may feel it is a waste of time, that many of the alternatives being promoted have already been considered and rejected, or agency managers simply don't want to have these alternatives considered. "Involving other agencies is bad enough, but involving citizens only muddies the decision process."

Political leaders also worry about losing control. They see a vocal community or a special interest group gain access to their political agenda and they say, "Why do these people have a greater say in the decision than others? I'm the elected official, so why do they (the stakeholders) have the limelight? Why are they being treated as if they have power and authority over this decision?"

- **Internal stakeholder conflict.** When citizen groups fight within and among themselves, focus on issues is lost. Public involvement means that all options, no matter how outlandish, self-serving or untested are explored. In this way, creative win-win resolution has the opportunity to be discovered. Resolution cannot occur if internal stakeholder group conflict keeps clear interests from being recognized. When internal conflict is present, control of the discussion is impossible. Nobody wins. The agency gets mixed messages and doesn't know who or what to believe. The decision gets delayed. To get beyond a stalemate, a compromise may be accepted that is in no one's best interest.

- **Fear of political launching pads.** "When ya get citizens involved in commissions, committees and decision making, ya never know where it may end. Hey, they may become the future mayors and council members...defeating us in elections."

Elected officials may be concerned that today's community leader will be tomorrow's political rival. Many up-and-coming politicians start as community rabble-rousers. In fact, one of the benefits of high quality community involvement is the ability to groom future elected and appointed officials.

- **Fear of media attention.** The media is always looking for a story with strong human interest, and nothing satisfies the viewer's appetite better than a David and Goliath article, with Goliath being the city hall bureaucrats. It is important to welcome the print media into the process from the very beginning. They will generally stay with a story from beginning to end and provide relative balance in the reporting. Electronic media, on the other hand, are usually on the prowl for a sound byte. By the end of thirty seconds, listeners want to have enough information to decide "who's right...who's wrong...and why did this awful bureaucracy do terrible things to these poor citizens?"

- **Early success.** Community involvement can generate surprising early success. When the shouting stops and people settle into civil discussions, the sponsor may think that the issue, project or problem is under control. At that point the agency may get complacent and return to their old ways of intuitive or staff-driven decision making. Leaving the citizen, resident and stakeholder out of the loop during the final stages of the process can be disastrous.

Tips for Future Community Involvement

With all the barriers to community involvement, how can an agency prepare the community, the staff and the policy makers for civic collaboration and civil discussion?

Establish clear process expectations that can apply to any public involvement process.

- Have a clear mission and set of objectives for the process. When the group digresses to discussions outside the mission, quickly bring them back.

- Negotiate ground rules with participants early in the process that bans personal attacks on character and motives.

- Explain there will be times during the community involvement process that progress will be difficult and slow going.

- Ask the group, the sponsor and staff to commit to process completion. Allow them to establish the criteria for success, failure and impasse. Honor those decisions.

- Set clear discussion boundaries—what's in the deal and what's outside the deal?

- When elected officials are concerned about creating their own political rivals, explain that such capacity building is the sign of a "statesman." It's part of their job to groom high quality replacements for themselves.

- If sponsors want to hurry a community involvement process, or claim victory before the full process is completed, remind them, "It ain't over 'til it's over."

Let everyone know that these public involvement committees have authority.

- Involve participants in the project design and the action plan. If they see weaknesses in the design or process, make changes to address the problems.

- Encourage the group's leaders to present final reports to elected and appointed policy makers. Give the stakeholders the credit they deserve.

- Honor their recommendations.

- Publicly and privately thank participants.

- At the beginning, the end and in the middle, show appreciation to participants for donating their time and energy to the process.

- Provide small, tangible tokens of appreciation that will be an ongoing reminder of their time together and the importance of their participation.

Create alternative ways for people to communicate.

- Establish an agency website to solicit ongoing interest in community involvement.

- Have the group select a steering committee to address changes during the community involvement process.

- Ask a few committee members to work directly with any concerned elected officials regarding the involvement process and the group's progress. When concerns are raised, these elected officials have a contact other than agency staff that can confirm or explain what's going on. These should not be substantive discussions of issues.

Make the media a partner.

- Long-term public involvement means having good access to media communications. They can be very helpful in preparing a community for a discussion. That means the agency actively solicits their participation from the very beginning. They need news...the agency needs ways to communicate. The media can be a partner in the community involvement process.

- It is to the agency's advantage to work with the media. Appearing open and forthright is always preferred to "no comment", which is never a good response to a question.

- The press will want a story on any controversial issue. Anticipate being contacted by media people. If possible, get ahead of the story by doing a press release on pending community involvement efforts. Find the reporter who frequently covers agency issues and educate them on public involvement policies.

- When speaking to the press, prepare three points about the process and substantive issues that the public needs to hear. Control the interview by bringing reporters back to those same points. If there isn't sufficient information to warrant a response to a question, indicate someone will follow up, and then do it.

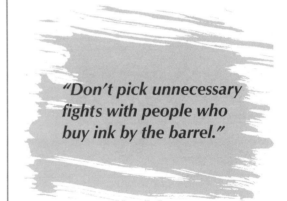

"Don't pick unnecessary fights with people who buy ink by the barrel."

Use strong, experienced facilitators to manage the process.

- Immediately enforce process agreements the first time a violation occurs.

- When internal conflict within a stakeholder group promises to halt the larger group's progress, meet with those in conflict "off line." Help them resolve their concerns so that the larger group can continue.

Things to Remember

- Create an ongoing constituency for public involvement.

- Develop institutional community involvement policies and procedures.

- There are significant barriers to instituting broad-based community involvement.

- Communication cannot be overemphasized.

Pros and Cons: Meeting Techniques

Tools	Descriptions	Pros	Cons
Workshops	▲ Held to achieve specific purpose ▲ Design attendance/agenda to maximize chances of achieving purpose ▲ Ideally limited to 12-25 people ▲ Agenda mailed prior to meeting ▲ Informal setting with open give and take discussion ▲ No formal process, no Robert's Rules of Order	▲ Effective in identifying problems ▲ Helps clarify key issues ▲ Good to search for a consensus	▲ Cost of preparation and materials ▲ Time required of staff and participants ▲ No public input outside of participants
Open Meetings	▲ An audience observes the meeting ▲ Mostly used by official public bodies bound by open meeting law ▲ Meeting and agenda publicly advertised ▲ Held at convenient time/location so affected interests can attend ▲ Formal meeting run by a chairman ▲ Must decide if and how public may participate in discussion	▲ Can establish legitimacy of agency ▲ Creates public record ▲ Public sees the officials in action ▲ Public sees which officials vote for or against the issue and hears their opinions ▲ Manageable	▲ Does not attempt to search for consensus ▲ Participants "play to the crowd" ▲ Remarks are guarded ▲ Limited public participation ▲ If meeting is mishandled, can destroy public confidence

Community Forums	▲ Designed to air certain issues when a decision has to be made soon but issues are not well enough understood ▲ Advertised widely ▲ Each affected interest makes a presentation ▲ Disinterested individual moderates ▲ Arrange TV and media coverage	▲ Exposes stakeholders to other views ▲ Helps staff to get to know stakeholders ▲ Helps staff see through the stakeholders' eyes ▲ Identifies problems and clarifies key issues	▲ Costly ▲ Time required by staff and participants
Public Hearings	▲ A formal setting to accept public comment ▲ Proceedings should consist of: summary of main points of problem; range of solutions; stakeholders' reaction to proposed solutions ▲ When you know opposition will be present, consider helping them prepare their presentation	▲ Official public record is made ▲ Minimal legal requirement for citizen participation ▲ Manageable	▲ Perfect setting for confrontation and conflict ▲ Citizens intimidated to speak ▲ Does not generate consensus ▲ Time required of staff and participants

Open Houses	▲ Informal setting allowing one-to-one exchanges ▲ Use public building people are familiar with and hold during convenient times ▲ Advertise widely through media and other channels ▲ Display possible solutions ▲ Have technical people present to answer questions on the spot ▲ Handouts of displays for people to take home for further examination ▲ Before leaving, people give written comments, suggestions and identify their preferred alternative and reasons	▲ Get to know stakeholders ▲ See through the stakeholders' eyes ▲ Nurtures credibility for agency/process ▲ Identifies problems ▲ Flexible format	▲ Costly ▲ Time required of staff ▲ Need to hold multiple open houses so all stakeholders have opportunity to attend ▲ Participants may not all receive information from one-to-one exchanges
Town Meetings	▲ Used to stay in touch with grass roots ▲ Must be well advertised ▲ Do not use for speech making ▲ Semi-formal setting ▲ People get a chance to see officials and ask a question ▲ Emphasis on active listening ▲ Resist answering all questions on the spot	▲ Good to hear views of stakeholders ▲ Establishes legitimacy of assumptions and earlier decisions ▲ Helps staff see issues through eyes of stakeholders	▲ Costly ▲ Time required of staff ▲ Risk of defending position ▲ If handled incorrectly can damage credibility

One-on-One Meetings	▲ Meet early in the planning process with stakeholders to determine their concerns and problems early enough to be resolved ▲ Include those who will be affected as well as those who perceive they will be affected ▲ Explain the project, why it is being developed, how it is being done, how far it has progressed and what is the schedule for decisions ▲ Invite the stakeholders to contribute views and solicit advice and comments ▲ Document the meeting ▲ Initial contact should be in writing	▲ Helps get to know stakeholders ▲ Creates public record of agency efforts ▲ Identifies problems ▲ Can open effective communication ▲ Effective in searching for a consensus	▲ Requires considerable on-going staff time ▲ Must be careful to avoid subjective selection of stakeholders

Pros and Cons: Communication Tools

Tools	Description	Pros	Cons
General Media			
News releases Media advisories Media briefings Legal notices Feature articles Letters to the editor Radio/TV appearances News conferences	▲ Convenient way to reach a great number of interests ▲ Must determine what purpose the communication is to achieve ▲ Consider carefully content and format ▲ Identify best method to achieve your purpose ▲ Be concise ▲ Clearly distinguish fact from opinion ▲ Avoid all jargon	▲ Low cost ▲ Flexible in presenting various messages ▲ Creates legitimacy of agency ▲ Helps agency clarify key issues for the public ▲ Nurture credibility ▲ Public more willing to trust if agency is open and presents all sides of an issue	▲ Lack of control over end product ▲ Potential for distorted message ▲ Not guaranteed coverage ▲ Could cause reporter to uncover new issues and side-track process ▲ Careless statements could be used against agency
Printed Materials			
Project Newsletter	▲ A brief, polished project news piece used to keep all stakeholders informed on how the project is progressing and new issues ▲ Must be published on a regular basis ▲ Maintain comprehensive mailing list of all stakeholders ▲ Do not use jargon ▲ Must contain real news of interest to the stakeholders ▲ Include any related news of interest even if it is not on the project ▲ Do not use as propaganda ▲ Report embarrassments, mistakes and controversies as well as good news ▲ Create a special introductory issue that can be mailed to new stakeholders throughout the project ▲ Remember to periodically clean up the mailing list	▲ Maintains legitimacy of the process ▲ Allows stakeholders to receive and understand communication ▲ Flexible to address changing issues	▲ Costly ▲ Time required of staff ▲ May appear to stakeholders as waste of public money if it doesn't contain real news

Tools	Description	Pros	Cons
Existing Newsletters - Company newsletters - Organization newsletters	▲ Piggy-back information with existing publications ▲ Identify the publications received by all stakeholders ▲ Be concise ▲ Articles must contain real news of interest to the readers ▲ Tailor information to the stakeholders which will receive the material ▲ Do not use jargon	▲ Time savings ▲ Cost savings ▲ Clarifies issues ▲ Stakeholders receive message through unbiased source ▲ Increases credibility of agency/process	▲ Lack of control ▲ Sometimes deadlines do not fit project schedule ▲ Subject to editing ▲ Material may not be used
Existing Internal Communications - Payroll inserts - Water bill mailers - Surveys - City Page	▲ Work with governments and employers to include flyers in mailings to employees and customers ▲ Must be concise ▲ Material must catch attention ▲ Try to put the message on company letterhead so people receive communication from unbiased third party ▲ Have questions related to project added to existing surveys	▲ Best for meeting notices ▲ Increase exposure to stakeholders ▲ Have communication received in an non-traditional manner	▲ Format restrictions ▲ Deadlines ▲ Distribution not guaranteed ▲ May be considered junk mail ▲ Could be costly if company requires payment based upon distribution numbers
Speakers Bureau			
Clubs **Civic Organizations** **Social Organizations** **Homeowners Association** **Schools** **Churches** **Chambers of Commerce** **PTA's** **Professional/Trade Organizations** **Major employers**	▲ Establish an on-going relationship with all existing organizations of each stakeholder ▲ Open up a two-way communication channel to get feedback from the group ▲ Make presentation or offer to participate in workshops, on panels, etc. ▲ Consider arranging a tour of the project for the group ▲ Inform members, don't try to get the organization to support	▲ Enables diverse groups to receive communication ▲ Low cost ▲ Clarifies key issues ▲ Identifies problems ▲ Helps to maintain legitimacy of the project/agency ▲ Nurtures credibility	▲ Time required of staff ▲ Project members get tired of chicken!

Tools	Description	Pros	Cons
Other Techniques			
Hotline Phone Number	▲ Used when a crash effort is needed ▲ Must follow through with the information received ▲ Must widely advertise number to be effective	▲ Quick easy communication link ▲ Some people want to talk to someone instead of writing a letter	▲ Assumes people will call ▲ Requires time to answer phone and follow-up ▲ Requires lead time to work with phone company to set up the line ▲ Can be costly
Survey	▲ Must decide what information you are looking for, what are you going to do with it, what specific questions you are trying to answer ▲ Be sure you can use the data that is collected ▲ Look for the information elsewhere first ▲ Survey should be statistically sound, brief, clear ▲ Pre-test the survey	▲ Systematic approach to getting data ▲ Establishes legitimacy of assumptions	▲ Costly ▲ Time required

Community Involvement Forms

Rules for a Good Meeting

Code of Cooperation & Responsiveness	Administrivia
✔ Critique ideas, not people…show respect for the views of others	✔ Where are the rest rooms and telephones?
✔ Ask honest questions	✔ Smoking???
✔ Make clear comments	✔ Room temperature
✔ Avoid side conversations	✔ Meeting breaks???
✔ Listen with an open mind	✔ You're not glued to your seat!!!
✔ Focus on functional, constructive controversy	✔ Pagers and cell phones
✔ Speak for yourself…own your words	✔ When in doubt, review these ground rules
✔ Everyone is responsible for advancing our agenda	✔ Pretend you're one hundred miles from home
	✔ What's the rule on confidentiality???
	✔ Thirty second soapbox?
	✔ Communicate effectively by actively listening
	✔ Make good decisions
	✔ Plan for action
	✔ Enjoy our time together

Meeting Evaluation Form

✛ Plus	▲ Delta

Questions to Ask at the End of the Meeting

Were the meeting objectives achieved as stated in the agenda? If so, why?   If not, why not?
        What was done to achieve the objectives?

What would be changed about this meeting if it were held again?

What specific actions should the leader take to improve the next meeting?

What specific actions should the participants take to improve the next meeting?

Action Plan Example

Action Plan		
What needs to be done?	Who is responsible?	When will it be complete?
Build ownership and buy-in in each of our own organizations	Everyone	Immediately
Process the meeting notes from the partnership meeting of 2/25 & 26/97	Mr. Decker	3/12/97
Distribute the meeting notes from the partnership meeting of 2/25 & 26/97	Mr. Nelson	3/15/97
Schedule and coordinate the first meeting of the coordinating committee	Ms. Babich	After 3/15/97
Develop coordinating committee meeting agenda	Ms. Babich and Mr. Nelson	After 3/15/97
Create a distribution of communication; provide fax, phone, mail and e-mail list	Mr. Nelson	3/15/97
Hold the first coordinating committee meeting	Coordinating Committee	No later than 4/4/97
Engage other potential partners in this effort	Coordinating Committee	After the first coordinating meeting
Develop a communication network & process protocol	Coordinating Committee	TBD
Create a resolution process	Coordinating Committee	TBD
Explore roles and authorities	Coordinating Committee	TBD
Develop the sub-group process to study all the areas developed in the substantive issues matrix	Coordinating Committee	TBD
Develop a priority list of substantive issues	Coordinating Committee	TBD

Meeting Planning Questionnaire

> **Meeting:**
> Who is the key contact for logistics in the agency? _____
> Who is the key contact for logistics at the facility? _____
> Phone number at meeting location: _____

The Human Dimensions

Who will be attending? Background information on attendees (resume, bio, etc.)
What are the relationships between participants? Supervisors-subordinate? Peers? Unrelated?
How safe will it be for people to participate? Physically? Emotionally?
What vehicles will be used to conduct discussions? Small groups? Group of the whole? Other?
How will participants prepare for the meeting?
Will there be formal work generated by the group that must be done after the meeting? Homework?
What is the group's role in decision making?
On what basis will the meeting be evaluated?
Who will judge the meeting's success?

How should conflict be managed? Aggression?
How should digression be managed?
Are there "land mines" that might derail the meeting? Sensitive issues?
Who or what might make this meeting fail?

The Meeting Content

What are the driving questions that must be answered? Subordinate questions?
What does the group know about the issues and the content of the discussions?
What are the discussion limits?
What hidden agendas might be working?
Is team-building a desired outcome of the meeting? Is so, what team issues are currently working?
What background materials must be supplied to participants at the meeting? In advance? Who is responsible for the advance mailing?

Meeting Logistics

The meeting will be held at:	
The date of the event is:	
Total number of participants:	
The meeting will start at: The meeting will end at: Breaks will occur at:	
Will food be served?	If yes, when will it be served and who is responsible?
Seating will be:	Who is responsible for setting up the room?
Equipment, meeting supplies and audio/visuals? Who will provide the equipment?	
Administrivia?	
Smoking?	
Limits of humor?	
Physical games and exercises?	
Rest rooms . . . phones . . . beepers?	

Stakeholder Identification List

Project: Revised:

Stakeholder Contact	Address	Phone/ Fax	Communication Techniques				
			Task Force	Newsletters	Focus Groups	One-on-One Meetings	Issue Map Interviewee

Messages

Common Messages and Themes

Sending Messages: What do you think the stakeholders need to know?

Message: Frequency   Means

_____   _____   _____
_____   _____   _____
                                                       _____   _____

Receiving Messages: What do the stakeholders think you need to know?

Message: Frequency   Means

_____   _____   _____
_____   _____   _____
                                                       _____   _____

Repeating Messages: The stakeholders have told us that...

Message: Frequency   Means

_____   _____   _____
_____   _____   _____
                                                       _____   _____

Verifying Messages: Our reliable sources hear that...

Message: Frequency   Means

_____   _____   _____
_____   _____   _____
_____   _____   _____

Key Questions to Ask When Dealing with Snipers

In the arena of community-based planning the term "sniper" refers to people who oppose a project or policy direction, but who intentionally hold themselves outside the formal citizen participation process. In some cases snipers have no interest in finding resolution to the issues on the table. Their sole purpose is to stalemate the decision or to create public conflict. In other instances the sniper's agenda is driven by a desire to challenge institutional direction and change policy direction. They believe their interests are best served by being an independent observer and critic of the process... to keep the public informed and the bureaucrats honest. In either case, snipers cause problems for people leading the process.

In addressing the problem of snipers, first try to understand why they remain outside formal discussions. It may be they were actually excluded from the process, or they felt they were not welcome. If so, find multiple points of entry for their energies and be inclusive.

If they choose to remain outside critics, identify key points of contention and determine if their issues warrant further consideration within the formal discussions. The simple act of acknowledging the sniper's opinions can go a long way toward conflict resolution.

The following are key questions you might ask to help develop a sniper response plan.

- Who are the snipers?
  - By name?
  - By affiliation?
  - Individuals working alone?
  - Loosely organized groups?
  - Closely coordinated groups?

- What issues do they raise?
  - Are their issues salient to the broader community?
  - Are their issues relevant to you?
  - Are their issues relevant to the topics you are addressing?
  - Are their issues tractable?

- What do the snipers hope to achieve by their actions?
  - Process failure?
  - Increased visibility?
  - Personal or corporate pain?
  - Institutional change?

- Do they hold credible positions and standing in the broader community?

- What methods might you use to draw the snipers into formal discussions?

- Are there leaders in the broader community who might challenge the sniper's agenda?
  - Formally?
  - Informally?

Appendix D:
Resources and a Reading List

Below, P. J., Morrisey, G. L., & Acomb, B. L. (1987). *The executive guide to strategic planning*. San Francisco: Jossey-Bass.

Benveniste, G. (1989). *Mastering the politics of planning*. San Francisco: Jossey-Bass.

Benzold, G. (Ed.). (1978). *Anticipatory democracy: People in the politics of the future*. New York: Vintage Books.

Bobo, K., Kendall, J., & Max, S. (1991). *Organizing for social change: A manual for activists, in the 90's*. Cabin John, MD: Seven Locks Press.

Carpenter, S. L., & Kennedy, W. J. D. (1988). *Managing Public Disputes*. San Francisco: Jossey-Bass.

Doyle, M., & Straus, D. (1982). *How to make meetings work*. New York: Jove Publications.

Folberg, J., & Taylor, A. (1984). *Mediation: A comprehensive guide to resolving conflicts without litigation*. San Francisco: Jossey-Bass.

Fox, W. M. (1987). *Effective group problem solving: How to broaden participation, improve decision making, and increase commitment to action.* San Francisco: Jossey-Bass.

Frank, M. O. (1989). *How to run a successful meeting in half the time.* New York: Pocket Books.

Institute for Participatory Management and Planning. (1993). *Citizen participation handbook for public officials and other professionals serving the public.* Monterey, CA: Author.

Kieffer, G. D. (1988). *The strategy of meetings.* New York: Warner Books.

London, Scott "Collaboration and Community", November, 1995, Pew Partnership for Civic Change.

Moore. C. W. (1986). *The mediation process: Practical strategies for resolving conflict.* San Francisco: Jossey-Bass.

Morris, J. A. (1994). *Not in my back yard: The handbook.* San Diego, CA: Silvercat Publications.

Nutt, P. C., & Backoff, R. W. (1992). *Strategic management of public and third sector organizations: A handbook for leaders.* San Francisco: Jossey-Bass.

Scholtes, P. R. (1992). *The team handbook: How to use teams to improve quality.* Madison, WI: Joiner Associates.

Schwarz, Roger M. (1994). *The skilled facilitator: Practical wisdome for developing effective groups.* San Francisco: Jossey-Bass.

Index

Order Form

Give the gift of *Over My Dead Body! A Workbook for Community Involvement* to all of your board/commission members and employees. Order additional copies here:

❏ YES, I want _____ copies of *Over My Dead Body! A Workbook for Community Involvement* at $29.95 U.S. plus $5.00 S&H (throughout the U. S. and Canada) Sales tax applies for all purchases in Arizona.

❏ YES, I am interested in having Lance Decker speak to my organization. Please contact me with details.

My check or money order for $ _____ is enclosed.
Please make your check payable to Lindworth Press

Please charge my:
❏ Visa ❏ MasterCard

Credit card # _____

Expiration date (month/year)_____/_____

Name_____

Organization_____

Address _____

City _____State _____Zip_____

Phone_____Fax_____

Email_____

Signature X_____

Return to:
Lindworth Press
5135 North 41st Place
Phoenix, AZ 85018-1664
www.lldecker.com
www.communityinvolvement.org
Email: ldecker@lldecker.com
Phone: 602.957.9659